Lillen Top
in Forget me not (120)
pattern on page 56

From left to right: **Gabrielle Jumper** in Peacock (144), **Gabrielle Jumper** in Fuchsia (143), **Gabrielle Jumper** in Daisy Yellow (142) pattern on page 40

CONTENTS

Nina Dress
in Putty Grey (121) pattern
on page 28

INTRODUCTION

At MillaMia we believe you can combine a love of knitting with a love of modern contemporary design and quality. That's why our patterns are inspired by the latest fashion trends, our colours are adapted seasonally and our yarn is made from the finest quality Merino wool. At the same time we really value our Scandinavian design heritage, and you will see this influence in our patterns.

In this book you will find 'The Close Knit Gang' collection, a range of patterns for both babies and children. While trend-influenced these designs are also shaped by a timeless, elegant vintage style, which means that they can be worn year-in year-out without appearing dated.

COLOUR IS SO IMPORTANT

We are very proud of the MillaMia colour range – our yarn is available in a great depth and intensity of colour. The colours in our range work together in a variety of combinations allowing you to create either a subtle tonal, or wonderful contrasting mix of colours.

The colours suggested in this book represent our vision, but the beauty of knitting is your ability to personalise the design to suit your child. If you look at our website, www.millamia.com, you will find a 'Colour Tool' that allows you to experiment, 'playing' with different combinations and making your own colour design decisions.

YOUR TIME MATTERS

Given the time investment of knitting an item, the final result should be something that is a delight to wear, that others will admire and that will last. Kids should want to wear it, which means it needs to be comfortable. So we've made sure our yarn is of the best quality, baby soft and yet can still be thrown into the machine for washing.

As knitters, we wanted a yarn that is easy and consistent to knit with. Forgiving and quick for beginners, yet fine enough to enable our patterns to achieve the best possible shape and stitch definition so as to reward more advanced knitters. The Naturally Soft Merino composition we have developed knits up wonderfully using the yarn either single or double, and our patterns take full advantage of this.

DESIGNS TO BE ENJOYED

We don't all have hours of time to spend on our knitting. That is why we've included a broad selection of patterns that range from easy to advanced, some shorter, some longer, some requiring extra techniques like cabling or colourwork and a variety of stitches.

Dip in, dip out, and if there is something you really love but feel you don't have the time or the skill to knit, set someone you know that loves knitting in the right direction with the pattern and yarn.

NEED SOME HELP?

If you are new to knitting or indeed a beginner who would like to try something a bit more challenging, our books are ideal for you. Log on to the 'Making Knitting Easy' section of our website, www.millamia.com, for more advice, or to download tools, post a question for our technical experts or indeed find someone who can help knit the item for you.

Despite numerous checks, occasionally there can be errors in knitting patterns. If you see what you think is an error the best thing is to visit www.millamia.com where any errors that have been spotted already will be published under 'Pattern Revisions'. If you cannot find the answer you are looking for, then do send an email or contact us via the website and we will get back to you as soon as possible to help.

BASIC INFORMATION

SKILL LEVELS

Recognising that we are not all expert knitters we have graded each pattern in the book to allow you to gauge whether it is one that you feel confident to try. The grades are as follows:

Beginner: You have just picked (or re-picked) up knitting needles and are comfortable with the basic concepts of knitting. By reading carefully you can follow a pattern. Items such as scarves and blankets and simple jumpers are ideal for you to start with.

Beginner / Improving: Having knitted a few pieces you are now looking to try new things, for instance colour combinations and features such as pockets. You might surprise yourself by trying some of the simpler colourwork or cable patterns in this book – you will find that they are not as difficult as you may have thought. Bear in mind that most experienced knitters will be happy to help a beginner so you can always ask for help too! Or look at our website for advice and help.

Improving: You have knitted a variety of items such as jumpers, cardigans and accessories in the past, and are comfortable with following patterns. You may have tried your hand at cable knitting and some form of colourwork before.

Experienced: You are comfortable with most knitting techniques. You have preferences and likes and dislikes, although are willing to try something new. You can read patterns quickly and are able to adapt them to your own requirements – for instance if resizing is needed.

YARN – SOME ADVICE

As there can be colour variations between dye lots when yarn is produced, we suggest that you buy all the yarn required for a project at the same time (with the same dye lot number) to ensure consistency of colour.

The amount of yarn required for each pattern is based on average requirements meaning they are an approximate guide.

The designs in this book have been created specifically with a certain yarn composition in mind. The weight, quality, colours, comfort and finished knit effect of this yarn is ideally suited to these patterns. Substituting for another yarn may produce a garment that is different from the design and images in this book.

For some of the heavier items in this book we have used a technique where we 'use the yarn double'. This simply means using two balls of yarn at once on a thicker needle (in our patterns a 5mm (US 8) needle) to produce a thicker quality to the knitted fabric. An advantage of this technique is that the garment will fly off your needles – being quick to knit up. Make sure you keep your two working balls of yarn spaced separately so that they do not tangle while knitting.

TENSION / GAUGE

A standard tension is given for all the patterns in this book. As the patterns are in different stitch types (e.g. stocking, garter, cable patterns, etc.) this tension may vary between patterns, and so you must check your tension against the recommendation at the start of the pattern. As matching the tension affects the final shape and size of the item you are knitting it can have a significant impact if it is not matched. Ensuring that you are knitting to the correct tension will result in the beautiful shape and lines of the original designs being achieved.

To check your tension we suggest that you knit a square according to the tension note at the start of each pattern (casting on an additional 10 stitches to the figure given in the tension note and knitting 5 to 10 more rows than specified in the tension note). You should knit the tension square in the stitch of the pattern (e.g. stocking, garter, cable pattern, etc).

Once knitted, mark out a 10 cm by 10 cm / 4 in by 4 in square using pins and count the number of stitches and rows contained within. If your tension does not quite match the one given try switching to either finer needles (if you have too few stitches in your square) or thicker needles (if you have too many stitches) until you reach the desired tension.

USEFUL RESOURCES

Visit your local yarn shop for MillaMia yarn or visit www.millamia.com to order directly or find local stockists. Shade cards can be ordered from our website as can the yarn and knitting needles. With our simple and modern website and express worldwide shipping, we aim to offer an easy, delightful and fun on-line experience.

We believe that using quality trims with our knitwear gives the garments a professional finishing touch. Most haberdashery shops and local yarn shops can provide great resources for these items.

SIZES

Instructions in the patterns are given for the smallest sizes and where they vary you should follow the figures in the brackets for larger sizes. If there is only one set of figures this means that they apply to all sizes.

Alongside the patterns in this book we give measurements for the items – as two children of the same age can have very different measurements, this can be used as a guide when choosing which size to knit and for checking your progress along the way. As age-sizing is not a precise science for children's clothing, the best way to ensure a good fit is to compare the actual garment measurements given in the pattern with the measurements of an existing garment that fits the child well. This will allow you to select the best size to knit the pattern in.

Please note that where a chest measurement is given in the table at the top of each pattern this refers to the total measurement of the garment **around** the chest. When the cross chest measurement is given graphically in the accompanying diagrams this is half the round chest measurement as it is simply measuring the distance across the front or back of the item, at chest level.

Children's clothes are by their nature looser fitting than adult wear and designed with plenty of 'ease' to make dressing and undressing less of an effort. This means that there is not as much shaping or fit to a child's garment as you will find in adult knitwear.

CARE OF YOUR GARMENT

See the ball band of MillaMia Naturally Soft Merino for washing and pressing instructions. Make sure you reshape your garments while they are wet after washing, and dry flat.

LANGUAGE

This book has been written in UK English. However, where possible US terminology has also been included and we have provided a translation of the most common knitting terms that differ between US and UK knitting conventions on page 9. In addition all sizes and measurements are given in both centimetres and inches throughout.

Remember that when a knitting pattern refers to the left and right sides of an item it is referring to the left or right side as worn, rather than as you are looking at it.

Gabrielle Jumper
in Daisy Yellow (142)
pattern on page 40

7

Alex Poncho
in Fawn (160)
pattern on page 82

ABBREVIATIONS

alt	alternate
approx	approximately
beg	begin(ning)
cont	continue
dec	decrease(ing)
foll	following
g-st	garter stitch
inc	increase(ing)
k or K	knit
k2 tog	knit two stitches together
m1	make one stitch by picking up the loop lying before the next stitch and knitting into back of it
m1p	make one stitch by picking up the loop lying before the next stitch and purling into back of it
mths	months
p or P	purl
p2 tog	purl two stitches together
p3 tog	purl three stitches together
patt	pattern
psso	pass slipped stitch over
pwise	purlwise
rib2 tog	rib two stitches together according to rib pattern being followed
rem	remain(ing)
rep	repeat(ing)
skpo	slip one, knit one, pass slipped stitch over – one stitch decreased
st(s)	stitch(es)
st st	stocking stitch
tbl	through back of loop
tog	together
yf	yarn forward
yo	yarn over
yon	yarn over needle to make a st
yrn	yarn round needle
y2rn	yarn twice round needle
[]	work instructions within brackets as many times as directed

UK AND US KNITTING TRANSLATIONS

UK	US
Cast off	Bind off
Colour	Color
Grey	Gray
Join	Sew
Moss stitch	Seed stitch
Tension	Gauge
Stocking stitch	Stockinette stitch
Yarn forward	Yarn over
Yarn over needle	Yarn over
Yarn round needle	Yarn over

KNITTING NEEDLE CONVERSION CHART

Metric, mm	US size
2	0
2.25	1
2.5	1
2.75	2
3	2
3.25	3
3.5	4
3.75	5
4	6
4.25	6
4.5	7
5	8
5.5	9
6	10
6.5	10.5
7	10.5
7.5	11
8	11
9	13
10	15

BJORN TANK TOP FREDRIK V-NECK

From left to right: **Bjorn Tank Top** in Claret (104) and Snow (124) pattern on page 12, **Fredrik V-Neck** in Moss (103) and Fawn (160) pattern on page 16, **Bjorn Tank Top** in Seaside (161) and Fawn (160) pattern on page 12

BJORN TANK TOP

SKILL LEVEL Beginner / Improving

SIZES / MEASUREMENTS

To fit age	3-6	6-9	9-12	12-24	24-36	mths

ACTUAL GARMENT MEASUREMENTS

Chest	42	45	48	55	61	cm
	16 ½	17 ½	19	21 ½	24	in
Length to	24	26	28	31	34	cm
shoulder	9 ½	10 ¼	11	12 ¼	13 ½	in

MATERIALS

- 2(2:2:3:3) 50g/1 ¾oz balls of MillaMia Naturally Soft Merino in Seaside (161) (M).
- One ball contrast colour in Fawn (160) (C).
- Pair each 3mm (US 2) and 3.25mm (US 3) knitting needles.
- Cable needle.

TENSION / GAUGE

25 sts and 34 rows to 10cm/4in over st st using 3.25mm (US 3) needles.
37 ½ sts and 34 rows to 10cm/4in over patt using 3.25mm (US 3) needles.

HINTS AND TIPS

A delightful tank top that really rewards trying new colour combinations. It is a manageable introduction to cable knitting for beginners who have not tried it before with just three simple cables on both the front and back. Style it on your favourite little boy with a simple white shirt and jeans for a modern yet classic look.

ABBREVIATIONS

C6F – cable 6 front, slip next 3 sts onto cable needle and hold at front of work, k3, then k3 from cable needle.
See also page 9.

SUGGESTED ALTERNATIVE COLOURWAYS

Fawn	Plum	Storm	Forget	Claret	Snow
160	162	102	me not	104	124
			120		

21 (22 ½ : 24 : 27 ½ : 30 ½) cm
8 ¼ (8 ¾ : 9 ½ : 10 ¾ : 12) in

24 (26 : 28 : 31 : 34) cm
9 ½ (10 ¼ : 11 : 12 ¼ : 13 ½) in

BACK

With 3mm (US 2) needles and C cast on 66(70:74:82:90) sts.
1st, 3rd, 4th and 5th sizes only
1st row P2, [k2, p2] to end.
2nd row K2, [p2, k2] to end.
2nd size only
1st row K2, [p2, k2] to end.
2nd row P2, [k2, p2] to end.
All sizes
These 2 rows form the rib.
Cont in rib working in stripes of 3(3:3:4:4) rows M, 3(3:3:4:4)
rows C, 3(3:3:4:4) rows M, 2 rows C, 1 row M, 2(2:2:3:3) rows C.
Change to 3.25mm (US 3) needles.
Cont in M only.
Cont in patt as folls:
1st row K16(18:20:24:28), p2, [C6F, p2, k2, p2] twice, C6F, p2,
k16(18:20:24:28).
2nd row P16(18:20:24:28), k2, [p6, k2, p2, k2] twice, p6, k2,
p16(18:20:24:28).
3rd row K16(18:20:24:28), p2, [k6, p2, k2, p2] twice, k6, p2,
k16(18:20:24:28).
4th row As 2nd row.
5th row As 3rd row.
6th row As 2nd row.
These 6 rows form the patt.
Cont in patt until back measures 14(15:16:19:21)cm/5 ½(6:6
¼:7 ½:8 ¼)in from cast on edge, ending with a wrong side row.
Shape armholes
Cast off 5(5:5:6:6) sts at beg of next 2 rows. 56(60:64:70:78) sts.**
Dec one st at each end of the next and 4(4:4:4:5) foll alt rows.
46(50:54:60:66) sts.
Cont in patt until back measures 24(26:28:31:34)cm/
9 ½(10 ¼:11:12 ¼:13 ½)in from cast on edge, ending with a
wrong side row.

Shape shoulders
Cast off 6(6:6:6:7) sts at beg of next 2 rows and 6(6:6:7:7) sts
at beg of foll 2 rows.
Leave rem 22(26:30:34:38) sts on a holder.

FRONT

Work as given for back to **.
Shape front neck
Next row Work 2 tog, patt 23(25:27:30:34) sts, work 2
tog, turn and work on these sts for first side of front neck.
25(27:29:32:36) sts.
Next row Patt to end.
Next row Work 2 tog, patt to last 2 sts, k2 tog.
Rep the last 2 rows 3(3:3:3:4) times. 17(19:21:24:26) sts rem.
Keeping armhole edge straight, dec one st at neck edge on
every foll alt row until 12(12:12:13:14) sts rem.
Cont straight until front measures same as back to shoulder,
ending at armhole edge.
Shape shoulder
Cast off 6(6:6:6:7) sts at beg of next row.
Work 1 row.
Cast off rem 6(6:6:7:7) sts.
With right side facing, slip centre 2 sts onto a safety pin, join
on yarn to rem sts.
Next row Skpo, patt to last 2 sts, work 2 tog.
Next row Patt to end.
Next row Skpo, patt to last 2 sts, work 2 tog.
Rep the last 2 rows 3(3:3:3:4) times. 17(19:21:24:26) sts rem.
Keeping armhole edge straight, dec one st at neck edge on
every foll alt row until 12(12:12:13:14) sts rem.
Cont straight until front measures same as back to shoulder,
ending at armhole edge.
Shape shoulder
Cast off 6(6:6:6:7) sts at beg of next row.
Work 1 row.
Cast off rem 6(6:6:7:7) sts.

NECKBAND

Join right shoulder seam.

With right side facing, using 3mm (US 2) needles and M, pick up and k36(36:40:46:48) sts evenly down left side of front neck, k2 from safety pin, pick up and k34(34:38:44:46) sts evenly up right side of front neck, patt 22(26:30:34:38) from back neck holder. 94(98:110:126:134) sts.

Change to C.

1st, 2nd, 3rd and 5th sizes only

1st row P2, * k2, p2; rep from * to end.

4th size only

1st row K2, * p2, k2; rep from * to end.

All sizes

This row sets the rib patt.

2nd row Starting rib patt with a p2 for the **4th size** and a k2 for **all other sizes**, rib 35(35:39:45:47), k2 tog, skpo, rib to end.

Change to M.

3rd row Rib to end.

Change to C.

4th row Rib 34(34:38:44:46), k2 tog, skpo, rib to end.

Using C cast off in rib.

ARMBANDS

Join left shoulder seam and neckband.

With right side facing, using 3mm (US 2) needles and M, pick up and k78(82:86:94:98) sts evenly around armhole edge.

Change to C.

1st row K2, * p2, k2; rep from * to end.

2nd row P2, * k2, p2; rep from * to end.

These 2 rows set the rib patt.

Work a further 1 row M, 1 row C.

Using C cast off in rib.

TO MAKE UP

Join side and armband seams.

FREDRIK V-NECK

SKILL LEVEL **Beginner / Improving**

SIZES / MEASUREMENTS

To fit age	3-6	6-12	12-24	24-36	36-48	48-60	mths

ACTUAL GARMENT MEASUREMENTS

Chest	51	56	61	66	70	75	cm
	20	22	24	26	27 ½	29 ½	in
Length to	25	27	30	33	37	41	cm
shoulder	10	10 ½	11 ¾	13	14 ½	16 ¼	in
Sleeve	15	17	19	22	25	28	cm
length	6	6 ¾	7 ½	8 ½	10	11	in

MATERIALS

- 3(3:4:4:5:6) 50g/1 ¾oz balls of MillaMia Naturally Soft Merino in Forget me not (120) (M).
- One ball contrast colour in Storm (102) (C).
- Pair each of 3mm (US 2) and 3.25mm (US 3) knitting needles.

TENSION / GAUGE

25 sts and 34 rows to 10cm/4in square over st st using 3.25mm (US 3) needles.

HINTS AND TIPS

A really classic v-neck that can be knitted in both baby and children's sizes. Subtle colour combinations ensure a stylish, simple end garment. Try it in more feminine colours for a girl.

ABBREVIATIONS

See page 9.

SUGGESTED ALTERNATIVE COLOURWAYS

Moss	Fawn	Snow	Seaside	Midnight	Claret
103	160	124	161	101	104

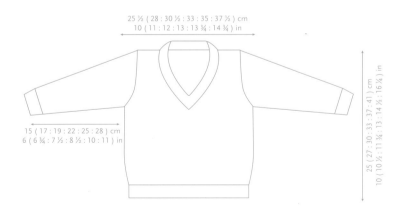

25 ½ (28 : 30 ½ : 33 : 35 : 37 ½) cm
10 (11 : 12 : 13 : 13 ¾ : 14 ¾) in

15 (17 : 19 : 22 : 25 : 28) cm
6 (6 ¾ : 7 ½ : 8 ½ : 10 : 11) in

25 (27 : 30 : 33 : 37 : 41) cm
10 (10 ½ : 11 ¾ : 13 : 14 ½ : 16 ¼) in

BACK

With 3mm (US 2) needles and C cast on 66(70:78:82:90:94) sts.
1st rib row K2, * p2, k2; rep from * to end.
2nd rib row P2, * k2, p2; rep from * to end.
Rep the last 2 rows 3(3:4:4:5:5) times more, inc 2 sts
evenly across last row on **2nd, 4th and 6th sizes only.**
66(72:78:84:90:96) sts.
Change to 3.25mm (US 3) needles.
Break off C.
Join on M.
Beg with a k row, cont in st st until back measures
15(16:18:20:23:26)cm/6(6 ¼:7:8:9:10 ¼)in from cast on edge,
ending with a p row.
Shape armholes
Cast off 3(3:4:4:5:5) sts at beg of next 2 rows.
60(66:70:76:80:86) sts. **
Next row K2, skpo, k to last 4 sts, k2tog, k2.
Next row P to end.
Rep the last 2 rows 2(3:3:4:4:5) times. 54(58:62:66:70:74) sts.
Cont in st st until back measures 25(27:30:33:37:41)cm/10(10
½:11 ¾:13:14 ½:16 ¼)in from cast on edge, ending with a p row.
Shape shoulders
Cast off 13(14:15:16:17:18) sts at beg of next 2 rows.
Leave rem 28(30:32:34:36:38) sts on a holder.

FRONT

Work as given for back to **.
Shape front neck
Next row K2, skpo, k21(24:26:29:31:34), k2tog, k2, turn and
work on these sts for first side of front neck.
Next row P to end.
Next row K2, skpo, k to last 4 sts, k2 tog, k2.
Rep the last 2 rows 1(2:2:3:3:4) times. 23(24:26:27:29:30) sts.
Keeping armhole edge straight cont to dec at neck edge on
every alt row until 13(14:15:16:17:18) sts rem.

Cont straight until front measures same as back to shoulder,
ending at armhole edge.
Cast off.
With right side facing, slip centre 2 sts onto a safety pin, join
on yarn to rem sts.
Next row K2, skpo, k to last 4 sts, k2 tog, k2.
Next row P to end.
Next row K2, skpo to last 4 sts, k2 tog, k2.
Rep the last 2 rows 1(2:2:3:3:4) times. 23(24:26:27:29:30) sts.
Keeping armhole edge straight cont to dec at neck edge on
every alt row until 13(14:15:16:17:18) sts rem.
Cont straight until front measures same as back to shoulder,
ending at armhole edge.
Cast off.

SLEEVES

With 3mm (US 2) needles and C cast on 38(38:42:42:46:46) sts.
1st rib row K2, * p2, k2; rep from * to end.
2nd rib row P2, * k2, p2; rep from * to end.
Rep the last 2 rows 3(3:4:4:5:5) times more, inc 2 sts
evenly across last row on **2nd, 4th and 6th sizes only.**
38(40:42:44:46:48) sts.
Change to 3.25mm (US 3) needles.
Break off C.
Join on M.
Beg with a k row, cont in st st.
Work 4(4:6:6:8:8) rows.
Inc row K3, m1, k to last 3 sts, m1, k3.
Work 3 rows.
Rep the last 4 rows 7(8:10:11:13:14) times more, and then the
inc row again.
56(60:66:70:76:80) sts.
Cont straight until sleeve measures 15(17:19:22:25:28)cm/
6(6 ¾:7 ½: 8 ½:10:11)in from cast on edge, ending with a p row.

Shape sleeve top

Cast off 3(3:4:4:5:5) sts at beg of next 2 rows.
50(54:58:62:66:70) sts.

Next row K2, skpo, k to last 4 sts, k2tog, k2.

Next row P to end.

Rep the last 2 rows 2(3:3:4:4:5) times. 44(46:50:52:56:58) sts.

Cast off 4 sts at beg of next 8(8:10:10:10:12) rows.

12(14:10:12:16:10) sts.

Cast off.

NECKBAND

Join right shoulder seam.

With right side facing, using 3mm (US 3) needles and C, pick up and k32(36:38:42:44:48) sts evenly down left side of front neck, k2 from safety pin, pick up and k32(34:38:40:44:46) sts evenly up right side of front neck, k28(30:32:34:36:38) sts from back neck holder. 94(102:110:118:126:134) sts.

1st, 2nd, 5th and 6th sizes only

1st row P2, [k2, p2] to end.

3rd and 4th sizes only

1st row K2, [p2, k2] to end.

All sizes

This row sets the rib.

2nd row Rib 31(35:37:41:43:47), k2 tog, skpo, rib to end.

3rd row Rib to end.

4th row Rib 30(34:36:40:42:46), k2 tog, skpo, rib to end.

5th row Rib to end.

6th row Rib 29(33:35:39:41:45), k2 tog, skpo, rib to end.

7th row Rib to end.

3rd, 4th, 5th and 6th sizes only

8th row Rib (34:38:40:44), k2 tog, skpo, rib to end.

9th row Rib to end.

5th and 6th sizes only

10th row Rib (39:43), k2 tog, skpo, rib to end.

11th row Rib to end.

All sizes

Cast off in rib, dec on this row as before.

TO MAKE UP

Join left shoulder seam and neckband. Join side and sleeve seams. Sew in sleeves.

MIKAEL
CARDIGAN
FREDRIK
V-NECK

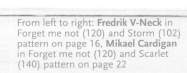

From left to right: **Fredrik V-Neck** in Forget me not (120) and Storm (102) pattern on page 16, **Mikael Cardigan** in Forget me not (120) and Scarlet (140) pattern on page 22

MIKAEL CARDIGAN

SKILL LEVEL Beginner / Improving

SIZES / MEASUREMENTS

To fit age	3-6	6-12	12-24	24-36	48-60	mths

ACTUAL GARMENT MEASUREMENTS

Chest	51	56	60	65	70	cm
	20	22	23 ½	25 ½	27 ½	in
Length to shoulder	24	26	28	32	36	cm
	9 ½	10 ¼	11	12 ½	14 ¼	in
Sleeve length	15	18	21	25	28	cm
	6	7	8 ¼	10	11	in

MATERIALS

- 3 (3:4:4:5) 50g/1 ¾oz balls of MillaMia Naturally Soft Merino in Forget me not (120) (M).
- One ball contrast colour in Scarlet (140) (C).
- Pair each of 3mm (US 2) and 3.25mm (US 3) knitting needles.
- Circular 3mm (US 2) knitting needle.
- 4 buttons (approx 15mm/⅝in diameter).

TENSION / GAUGE

25 sts and 34 rows to 10cm/4in square over st st using 3.25mm (US 3) needles.

HINTS AND TIPS

A relaxed fit cardigan that works well for both boys and girls.

ABBREVIATIONS

See page 9.

SUGGESTED ALTERNATIVE COLOURWAYS

Midnight 101   Grass 141

Fawn 160   Peacock 144

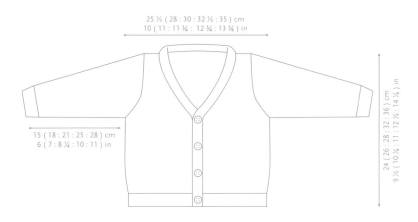

25 ½ (28 : 30 : 32 ½ : 35) cm
10 (11 : 11 ¾ : 12 ¾ : 13 ¾) in

15 (18 : 21 : 25 : 28) cm
6 (7 : 8 ¼ : 10 : 11) in

24 (26 : 28 : 32 : 36) cm
9 ½ (10 ¼ : 11 : 12 ½ : 14 ¼) in

BACK

With 3mm (US 2) needles and C cast on 66(70:78:82:90) sts.
1st rib row K2, [p2, k2] to end.
2nd rib row P2, [k2, p2] to end.
Rep the last 2 rows 3(3:4:4:5) times more, inc 2 sts across last row on **2nd and 4th sizes only.** 66(72:78:84:90) sts.
Cut off C.
Join on M.
Change to 3.25mm (US 3) needles.
Beg with a k row, cont in st st until back measures 14(15:16:19:22)cm/5 ½(6:6 ¼:7 ½:8 ¾)in from cast on edge, ending with a p row.
Shape armholes
Cast off 3(3:3:4:4) sts at beg of next 2 rows. 60(66:72:76:82) sts.
Next row K2, skpo, k to last 4 sts, k2 tog, k2.
Next row P to end.
Rep the last 2 rows 3(4:5:5:6) times. 52(56:60:64:68) sts.
Cont in st st until back measures 24(26:28:32:36)cm/9 ½ (10 ¼:11:12 ½:14 ¼)in from cast on edge, ending with a p row.
Shape shoulders
Cast off 6(6:7:7:8) sts at beg of next 2 rows and 6(7:7:8:8) sts at beg of foll 2 rows.
Leave rem 28(30:32:34:36) sts on a holder.

LEFT FRONT

With 3mm (US 2) needles and C cast on 31(35:35:39:43) sts.
1st rib row K2, [p2, k2] to last 5 sts, p2, k3.
2nd rib row P3, [k2, p2] to end.
Rep the last 2 rows 3(3:4:4:5) times more, dec 1 st at centre of last row on **2nd size only** and inc (2:1) sts across row on **(3rd:4th) sizes only.** 31(34:37:40:43) sts.
Cut off C.
Join on M.
Change to 3.25mm (US 3) needles.

Beg with a k row, cont in st st until front measures 14(15:16:19:22)cm/5 ½(6:6 ¼:7 ½:8 ¾)in from cast on edge, ending with a p row.
Shape armhole and front neck
Cast off 3(3:3:4:4) sts at beg of next row. 28(31:34:36:39) sts.
Next row P to end.
Next row K2, skpo, k to last 4 sts, k2 tog, k2.
Next row P to end.
Rep the last 2 rows 3(4:5:5:6) times. 20(21:22:24:25) sts.
Keeping armhole edge straight cont to dec at neck edge on every right side row until 12(13:14:15:16) sts rem.
Work straight until front matches back to shoulder, ending at armhole edge.
Shape shoulder
Cast off 6(6:7:7:8) sts at beg of next row.
Work 1 row.
Cast off rem 6(7:7:8:8) sts.

RIGHT FRONT

With 3mm (US 2) needles and C cast on 31(35:35:39:43) sts.
1st rib row K3, [p2, k2] to end.
2nd rib row P2, [k2, p2] to last 5 sts, k2, p3.
Rep the last 2 rows 3(3:4:4:5) times more, dec 1 st at centre of last row on **2nd size only** and inc (2:1) sts across row on **(3rd:4th) sizes only.** 31(34:37:40:43) sts.
Cut off C.
Join on M.
Change to 3.25mm (US 3) needles.
Beg with a k row, cont in st st until front measures 14(15:16:19:22)cm/5 ½(6:6 ¼:7 ½:8 ¾)in from cast on edge, ending with a k row.
Shape armhole and front neck
Cast off 3(3:3:4:4) sts at beg of next row. 28(31:34:36:39) sts.
Next row K2, skpo, k to last 4 sts, k2 tog, k2.
Next row P to end.
Rep the last 2 rows 3(4:5:5:6) times. 20(21:22:24:25) sts.

Keeping armhole edge straight cont to dec at neck edge on every right side row until 12(13:14:15:16) sts rem.
Work straight until front matches back to shoulder, ending at armhole edge.

Shape shoulder

Cast off 6(6:7:7:8) sts at beg of next row.

Work 1 row.

Cast off rem 6(7:7:8:8) sts.

SLEEVES

With 3mm (US 2) needles and C cast on 34(34:38:38:42) sts.

1st rib row K2, [p2, k2] to end.

2nd rib row P2, [k2, p2] to end.

Rep the last 2 rows 3(3:4:4:5) times more, inc 2 sts evenly across last row on **2nd and 4th sizes only**. 34(36:38:40:42) sts.

Cut off C.

Join on M.

Change to 3.25mm (US 3) needles.

Beg with a k row, cont in st st.

Work 6 rows.

Inc row K3, m1, k to last 3 sts, m1, k3.

Work 3 rows.

Rep the last 4 rows 5(7:9:11:13) times more, and then the inc row again. 48(54:60:66:72) sts.

Cont straight until sleeve measures 15(18:21:25:28)cm/ 6(7:8 ¼:10:11)in from cast on edge, ending with a p row.

Shape sleeve top

Cast off 3(3:3:4:4) sts at beg of next 2 rows. 42(48:54:58:64) sts.

Next row K2, skpo, k to last 4 sts, k2 tog, k2.

Next row P to end.

Rep the last 2 rows 3(4:5:5:6) times. 34(38:42:46:50) sts.

Cast off 2 sts at beg of next 10(10:12:12:14) rows.

14(18:18:22:22) sts.

Cast off rem sts.

FRONT BAND

Join shoulder seams.

With right side facing, 3mm (US 2) circular needle and C, pick up and k35(38:43:47:51) sts up right front edge, to beg of neck shaping, 28(30:34:37:40) sts along right front neck edge, 28(30:32:34:36) sts from back neck, pick up and k28(30:34:37:40) sts down left front neck edge to beg of neck shaping, 35(38:43:47:51) along left front edge. 154(166:186:202:218) sts.

1st rib row P2, * k2, p2; rep from * to end.

2nd rib row K2, * p2, k2; rep from * to end.

Rib 1 more row.

Girl's version

Buttonhole row Rib 3, [yrn, rib 2 tog, rib 8(9:10:11:12)] 3 times, yrn, rib2 tog, rib to end.

Boy's version

Buttonhole row Rib 119(128:145:158:171), [rib 2 tog, yrn, rib 8(9:10:11:12)] 3 times, rib 2 tog, yrn, rib 3.

Both versions

Rib 3 more rows.

Cast off in rib.

TO MAKE UP

Join side and sleeve seams. Sew in sleeves. Sew on buttons.

NINA DRESS SOFIA POLO NECK

From left to right: **Nina Dress** in Plum
(162) pattern on page 28, **Sofia Polo
Neck** in Storm (102) pattern on page 34

NINA DRESS

SKILL LEVEL **Improving**

SIZES / MEASUREMENTS

To fit age	1-2	2-3	3-4	4-5	years

ACTUAL GARMENT MEASUREMENTS

Chest	57	62	67	72	cm
	22 ½	24 ½	26 ½	28½	in
Length to shoulder	45	50	56	64	cm
	17 ¾	19 ¾	22	25	in
Sleeve length	8	9	10	11	cm
	3	3 ½	4	4 ½	in

MATERIALS

• 5(6:7:7) 50g/1 ¾oz balls MillaMia Naturally Soft Merino in Plum (162).
• Pair each 3mm (US 2) and 3.25mm (US 3) needles.
• 140cm/55in ribbon (approx 25mm/1in wide).

TENSION / GAUGE

25 sts and 34 rows to 10cm/4in square over st st using 3.25mm(US 3) needles.

HINTS AND TIPS

A beautiful, elegant dress. By ensuring that you knit this item to the required tension you will achieve the simple, neat shape of the design. Try teaming it with different ribbons in either a matching shade in satin or contrast grosgrain to vary the finished effect. Knit the Louise Headband to match and use up any leftover yarn.

ABBREVIATIONS

See page 9.

SUGGESTED ALTERNATIVE COLOURWAYS

Putty Grey 121	Midnight 101	Seaside 161	Lilac Blossom 123	Claret 104

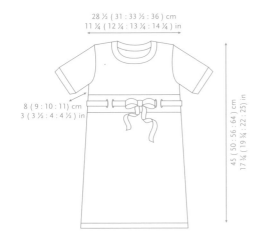

28 ½ (31 : 33 ½ : 36) cm
11 ¼ (12 ¼ : 13 ¼ : 14 ¼) in

8 (9 : 10 : 11) cm
3 (3 ½ : 4 : 4 ½) in

45 (50 : 56 : 64) cm
17 ¾ (19 ¾ : 22 : 25) in

BACK

With 3.25mm (US 3) needles cast on 98(110:122:134) sts.
1st row P2, [k4, p2] to end.
2nd row K2, [p4, k2] to end.
Rep the last 2 rows twice more.
Beg with a k row cont in st st.
Work 2 rows.
Dec row K4, skpo, k to last 6 sts, k2 tog, k4.
Work 5 rows.
Rep the last 6 rows 10(13:16:19) times more, and then the dec row again. 74(80:86:92) sts.
Work straight until back measures 25(29:34:41)cm/10(11 ½: 13 ½:16 ¼)in from cast on edge, ending with a wrong side row.
1st row P2, [k4, p2] to end.
2nd row K2, [p4, k2] to end.
These 2 rows form the rib.
Work a further 6 rows.
Next row Rib 14(14:20:20), turn and work 6 rows on these sts, break off yarn, rejoin yarn to next st, k4, turn, [k1, p2, k1, turn, k4, turn] 3 times, break off yarn, rejoin yarn to next st, rib 38(44:38:44), turn and work 6 rows on these sts, break off yarn rejoin yarn to next st, k4, turn, [k1, p2, k1, turn, k4, turn] 3 times, break off yarn, rejoin yarn to next st, rib 14(14:20:20), turn and work 6 rows on these sts.
Next row Rib across all sts.
Work a further 8 rows in rib.
Beg with a k row cont in st st until back measures 35(39:44:51) cm/13 ¾(15 ½:17 ½: 20)in from cast on edge, ending with a wrong side row.
Shape armholes
Cast off 4(5:6:7) sts at beg of next 2 rows. 66(70:74:78) sts.
Next row K2, skpo, k to last 4 sts, k2 tog, k2.
Next row P to end.
Rep the last 2 rows 6 times more. 52(56:60:64) sts.
Cont in st st until back measures 43(48:54:62 cm/17(19:21 ¼: 24 ½)in from cast on edge, ending with a wrong side row.

Shape back neck
Next row K15(17:18:19) sts, turn and work on these sts.
Dec one st at neck edge on next 4 rows. 11(13:14:15) sts.
Work 1 row.
Shape shoulder
Cast off 5(6:7:7) sts at the beg of next row.
Work 1 row.
Cast off rem 6(7:7:8) sts.
With right side facing slip centre 22(22:24:26) sts on a holder, rejoin yarn to rem sts, k to end.
Dec one st at neck edge on next 4 rows. 11(13:14:15) sts.
Work 2 rows.
Shape shoulder
Cast off 5(6:7:7) sts at the beg of next row.
Work 1 row.
Cast off rem 6(7:7:8) sts.

FRONT

Work as given for back until front measures 39(44:49:56)cm/ 15 ¼(17 ¼:19 ¼:22)in from cast on edge, ending with a wrong side row. 52(56:60:64) sts.
Shape front neck
Next row K19(21:22:24), turn and work on these sts.
Dec one st at neck edge on next 8(8:8:9) rows. 11(13:14:15) sts.
Work straight until front measures same as back to shoulder shaping, ending at armhole edge.
Shape shoulder
Cast off 5(6:7:7) sts at the beg of next row.
Work 1 row.
Cast off rem 6(7:7:8) sts.
With right side facing slip centre 14(14:16:16) sts on a holder, rejoin yarn to rem sts, k to end.
Dec one st at neck edge on next 8(8:8:9) rows. 11(13:14:15) sts.

Work straight until front measures same as back to shoulder shaping, ending at armhole edge.

Shape shoulder

Cast off 5(6:7:7) sts at the beg of next row.

Work 1 row.

Cast off rem 6(7:7:8) sts.

SLEEVES

With 3mm (US 2) needles cast on 50(56:62:68) sts.

1st row P2, [k4, p2] to end.

2nd row K2, [p4, k2] to end.

Rep the last 2 rows twice more.

Change to 3.25mm (US 3) needles.

Beg with a k row cont in st st.

Work 2 rows.

Inc row K4, m1, k to last 4 sts, m1, k4.

Work 5 (7:9:11) rows.

Inc row K4, m1, k to last 4 sts, m1, k4. 54(60:66:72) sts.

Cont straight until sleeve measures 8(9:10:11)cm/3(3 ½:4:4 ½)in from cast on edge, ending with a p row.

Shape top

Cast off 4(5:6:7) sts at beg of next 2 rows. 46(50:54:58) sts.

Next row K2, skpo, k to last 4 sts, k2 tog, k2.

Next row P to end.

Rep the last 2 rows 9(10:11:12) times. 26(28:30:32) sts.

Cast off 3 sts at beg of next 6 rows.

Cast off rem 8(10:12:14) sts.

NECKBAND

Join right shoulder seam.

With 3mm (US 2) needles pick up and k22(22:23:25) sts down left side of front neck, k14(14:16:16) sts on front neck holder, pick up and k22(22:23:25) sts up right side of front neck, 9 sts down right side of back neck, k22(22:24:26) sts on back neck holder, pick up and k9 sts up left side of back neck. 98(98:104:110) sts.

1st row K2, [p4, k2] to end.

2nd row P2, [k4, p2] to end.

Rep the last 2 rows once more and the 1st row again.

Cast off in rib.

TO MAKE UP

Join side and sleeve seams. Sew in sleeves. Thread ribbon through loops to tie at front.

LOUISE HEADBAND

SKILL LEVEL **Beginner / Improving**

SIZES / MEASUREMENTS

To fit age   One size

ACTUAL MEASUREMENT

All round   43cm/17in by 5.5cm/2 ¼in wide.

MATERIALS

- One 50g/1 ¾oz ball of MillaMia Naturally Soft Merino in Plum (162) (M).
- Small amount in Storm Grey (102) (C).
- Pair 3.25mm (US 3) needles.
- 100cm/39in length of ribbon (approx 25mm/1in wide).

TENSION / GAUGE

28 sts and 36 rows to 10cm/4in square over rib slightly stretched using 3.25mm (US 3) needles.

HINTS AND TIPS

A great way to use up leftover yarn from either the Sofia Polo Neck or Nina Dress that creates a wonderful matching accessory. You could start by knitting this headband to practice making the ribbon holes that feature also on Sofia and Nina.

ABBREVIATIONS

See page 9.

SUGGESTED ALTERNATIVE COLOURWAYS

Lilac Blossom 123   Midnight 101   Snow 124   Fawn 160

TO MAKE

With 3.25mm (US 3) needles and C cast on 122 sts.
1st row P2, [k4, p2] to end.
2nd row K2, [p4, k2] to end.
These 2 rows form the rib.
Work 1 more row.
Cut off C.
Join on M.
Work a further 3 rows.
Next row Rib 14, turn and work 6 rows on these sts, break off yarn, ** rejoin yarn to next st, k4, turn, [k1, p2, k1, turn, k4, turn] 3 times, break off yarn, rejoin yarn to next st, rib 26, turn and work 6 rows on these sts, break off yarn; rep from ** twice more, rejoin yarn to next st, k4, turn, [k1, p2, k1, turn, k4, turn] 3 times, break off yarn, rejoin yarn to next st, rib 14, turn and work 6 rows on these sts.

Next row Rib across all sts.
Work a further 3 rows.
Cut off M.
Join on C.
Work a further 3 rows.
Cast off in rib.

TO COMPLETE

Join seam. Thread ribbon through loops to tie at centre front.

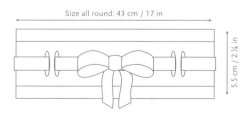

Size all round: 43 cm / 17 in

5.5 cm / 2 ¼ in

SOFIA POLO NECK

SKILL LEVEL **Improving**

SIZES / MEASUREMENTS

To fit age	3-4	4-5	5-6	years

ACTUAL GARMENT MEASUREMENTS

Chest	64	70	77	cm
	25	27 ½	30 ½	in
Length to shoulder	39	44	49	cm
	15 ¼	17 ¼	19 ¼	in
Sleeve length	22	25	28	cm
	8 ½	9 ¾	11	in

MATERIALS

- 6(7:7) 50g/1 ¾oz balls of MillaMia Naturally Soft Merino in Storm (102).
- Pair each 3mm (US 2) and 3.25mm (US 3) needles.
- 140cm/55in ribbon (approx 25mm/1in wide).

TENSION / GAUGE

25 sts and 34 rows to 10cm/4in square over st st using 3.25mm (US 3) needles.

HINTS AND TIPS

A sleek slim-fitting polo neck with a deliberately loose rib neck that children will not object to wearing. By making sure that you knit this item to the required tension you will achieve the elegant fit of the design. A satin ribbon makes it more glamorous while a contrast grosgrain colour ribbon can make the design more casual. Knit the Louise Headband to match and use up any leftover yarn.

ABBREVIATIONS

See page 9.

SUGGESTED ALTERNATIVE COLOURWAYS

Midnight	Plum	Fawn	Moss
101	162	160	103

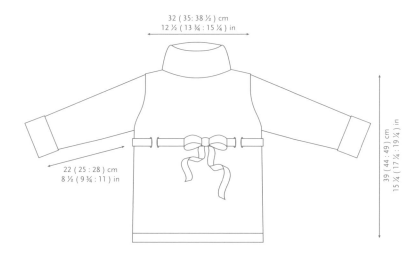

32 (35: 38 ½) cm
12 ½ (13 ¾ : 15 ¼) in

22 (25 : 28) cm
8 ½ (9 ¾ : 11) in

39 (44 : 49) cm
15 ¼ (17 ¼ : 19 ¼) in

BACK

With 3.25mm (US 3) needles cast on 82(90:98) sts.
1st row K3, [p4, k4] to last 7 sts, p4, k3.
2nd row P3, [k4, p4] to last 7 sts, k4, p3.
Rep the last 2 rows 3 times more.
Beg with a k row cont in st st until back measures 22(26:30)cm/
8 ¾(10 ¼:11 ¾)in from cast on edge, ending with a p row.
Next row K12(14:16), turn, [k1, p11(13:15), turn, k12(14:16),
turn] 3 times, break off yarn, rejoin yarn to next st, k4, turn, [k1,
p2, k1, turn, k4, turn] 3 times, break off yarn, rejoin yarn to next
st, k50(54:58) turn, [k1, p48(52:56), k1, turn, k50(54:58) turn]
3 times, break off yarn, rejoin yarn to next st, k4, turn, [k1, p2,
k1, turn, k4, turn] 3 times, break off yarn, rejoin yarn to next st,
k12(14:16), turn, [p11(13:15), k1, turn, k12(14:16), turn] 3 times.
Next row P across all sts.
Beg with a k row cont in st st until back measures 27(31:35)cm/
10 ¾(12 ¼:13 ¾)in from cast on edge, ending with a p row.
Shape armholes
Cast off 6(7:8) sts at beg of next 2 rows. 70(76:82) sts.
Next row K3, skpo, k to last 5 sts, k2 tog, k3.
Next row P to end.
Rep the last 2 rows 6(7:8) times more. 56(60:64) sts.
Work straight until back measures 37(42:47)cm/14 ½(16 ½:
18 ½)in from cast on edge, ending with a p row.
Shape back neck
Next row K18(19:20), turn and work on these sts.
Dec one st at neck edge on next 4 rows. 14(15:16) sts.
Work 1 row.
Shape shoulder
Cast off 7(7:8) sts at the beg of next row.
Work 1 row.
Cast off rem 7(8:8) sts.
With right side facing slip centre 20(22:24) sts on a holder,
rejoin yarn to rem sts, k to end.
Dec one st at neck edge on next 4 rows. 14(15:16) sts.
Work 2 rows.

Shape shoulder
Cast off 7(7:8) sts at the beg of next row.
Work 1 row.
Cast off rem 7(8:8) sts.

FRONT

Work as given for back until front measures 35(39:43)cm/
13 ¾(15 ¼:17)in from cast on edge, ending with a p row.
Shape front neck
Next row K20(21:22), turn and work on these sts.
Dec one st at neck edge on next 6 rows. 14(15:16) sts.
Work straight until front measures same as back to shoulder
shaping, ending at armhole edge.
Shape shoulder
Cast off 7(7:8) sts at the beg of next row.
Work 1 row.
Cast off rem 7(8:8) sts.
With right side facing slip centre 16(18:20) sts on a holder,
rejoin yarn to rem sts, k to end.
Dec one st at neck edge on next 6 rows. 14(15:16) sts.
Work straight until front measures same as back to shoulder
shaping, ending at armhole edge.
Shape shoulder
Cast off 7(7:8) sts at the beg of next row.
Work 1 row.
Cast off rem 7(8:8) sts.

SLEEVES

With 3.25mm (US 3) needles cast on 50(58:66) sts.
1st row K3, [p4, k4] to last 7 sts, p4, k3.
2nd row P3, [k4, p4] to last 7 sts, k4, p3.
Rep the last 2 rows 10(11:12) times more and the 1st row again.
Change to 3mm (US 2) needles.
Mark each end of last row with a coloured thread.
Starting with a 1st row, work a further 22(24:26) rows in rib.

Change to 3.25mm (US 3) needles.
Work 4 rows st st.
Inc row K3, m1, k to last 3 sts, m1, k3.
Work 11(13:15) rows.
Rep the last 12(14:16) rows twice more, and then the inc row
again. 58(66:74) sts.
Cont straight until sleeve measures 22(25:28)cm/8 ½(9 ¾:11)in
from coloured thread, ending with a p row.
Shape sleeve top
Cast off 6(7:8) sts at beg of next 2 rows. 46(52:58) sts.
Next row K2, skpo, k to last 4 sts, k2 tog, k2.
Next row P to end.
Rep the last 2 rows 9(10:11) times more. 26(30:34) sts.
Cast off 3 sts at beg of next 6 rows.
Cast off rem 8(12:16) sts.

COLLAR

Join right shoulder seam.
With 3mm (US 2) needles pick up and k20(22:24) sts down
left side of front neck, k16(18:20) sts on front neck holder, pick
up and k20(22:24) sts up right side of front neck, 11 sts down
right side of back neck, k20(22:24) sts on back neck holder,
pick up and k11 sts up left side of back neck. 98(106:114) sts.
1st row K3, [p4, k4] to last 7 sts, p4, k3.
2nd row P3, [k4, p4] to last 7 sts, k4, p3.
Rep the last 2 rows 9(10:11) times more and the 1st row again.
Change to 3.25mm (US 3) needles.
Starting with a 1st row, work a further 22(24:26) rows in rib.
Cast off in rib.

TO MAKE UP

Reversing neckband and cuff seams to fold back, join left
shoulder and neckband seam then join side and sleeve seams.
Sew on sleeves. Thread ribbon through loops to tie at front.

GABRIELLE
JUMPER

From left to right: **Gabrielle Jumper** in
Peacock (144), **Gabrielle Jumper** in Fuchsia
(143), **Gabrielle Jumper** in Daisy Yellow (142)
pattern on page 40

GABRIELLE JUMPER

SKILL LEVEL **Experienced**

SIZES / MEASUREMENTS

To fit age	0-6	6-12	12-24	24-36	48-60	mths

ACTUAL GARMENT MEASUREMENTS

Chest	55	62	67	75	80	cm
	21 ½	24 ½	26 ½	29 ½	31 ½	in
Length to	26	28	30	33	36	cm
shoulder	10 ¼	11	11 ¾	13	14 ¼	in
Sleeve	16	19	22	25	28	cm
length	6 ¼	7 ½	8 ½	9 ¾	11	in

MATERIALS

• 4(4:5:6:7) 50g/1 ¾oz balls of MillaMia Naturally Soft Merino in Fuchsia (143).
• Pair each 3mm (US 2) and 3.25mm (US 3) knitting needles.
• Cable needle.
• 3 small buttons (approx 12mm/½in diameter).

TENSION / GAUGE

32 sts and 38 rows to 10cm/4in square over patt slightly stretched using 3.25mm (US 3) needles.

HINTS AND TIPS

The delicate, small cables look and feel delightful once knitted, and the pattern works really well in bright colours. Making it will pass many an evening for the dedicated knitter.

ABBREVIATIONS

C4F – slip next 2 sts onto cable needle and hold at front of work, k2, then k2 from cable needle.
m1p – make one st by picking up and purling into back of loop between st just worked and next st.
See also page 9.

SUGGESTED ALTERNATIVE COLOURWAYS

Scarlet	Grass	Daisy	Peacock	Lilac Blossom
140	141	142	144	123

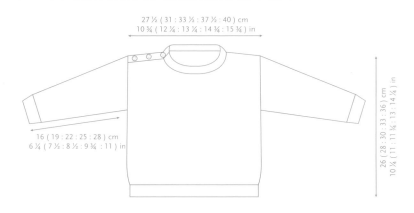

27 ½ (31 : 33 ½ : 37 ½ : 40) cm
10 ¾ (12 ¼ : 13 ¼ : 14 ¾ : 15 ¾) in

16 (19 : 22 : 25 : 28) cm
6 ¼ (7 ½ : 8 ½ : 9 ¾ : 11) in

26 (28 : 30 : 33 : 36) cm
10 ¼ (11 : 11 ¾ : 13 : 14 ¼) in

BACK

With 3mm (US 2) needles cast on 74(82:90:98:106) sts.
1st row (right side) K2, * p2, k2; rep from * to end.
2nd row P2, * k2, p2; rep from * to end.
Rep the last 2 rows 3 times more and the first row again.
Inc row (wrong side) P2, k2(0:2:0:2), p2(0:2:0:2), * k2, m1p,
p2, m1p, k2, p2; rep from * to last 4(0:4:0:4) sts, k2(0:2:0:2),
p2(0:2:0:2). 90(102:110:122:130) sts.
Change to 3.25mm (US 3) needles.
Work in patt as follows:
1st row K2, p2(0:2:0:2), k2(0:2:0:2), * p2, k4, p2, k2; rep from *
to last 4(0:4:0:4) sts, p2(0:2:0:2), k2(0:2:0:2).
2nd row P2, k2(0:2:0:2), p2(0:2:0:2), * k2, p4, k2, p2; rep from
* to last 4(0:4:0:4) sts, k2(0:2:0:2), p2(0:2:0:2).
3rd row K2, p2(0:2:0:2), k2(0:2:0:2), * p2, C4F, p2, k2; rep
from * to last 4(0:4:0:4) sts, p2(0:2:0:2), k2(0:2:0:2).
4th row As 2nd row.
5th row K2, p2(0:2:0:2), k2(0:2:0:2), * p2, k4, p2, k2; rep from *
to last 4(0:4:0:4) sts, p2(0:2:0:2), k2(0:2:0:2).
6th row As 2nd row.
These 6 rows form the patt.
Cont in patt until back measures 15(16:17:19:21)cm/6(6 ¼:
6 ¾:7 ½:8 ¼)in from cast on edge, ending with a wrong side row.
Shape armholes
Cast off 3 sts at beg of next 2 rows. 84(96:104:116:124) sts.
Cont in patt until back measures 26(28:30:33:36)cm/
10 ¼(11:11 ¾:13:14 ¼)in from cast on edge, ending with a
wrong side row.
Shape shoulders
Next row Patt 13(15:16:18:19) sts, place these sts on a holder,
patt to end.
Next row Cast off 13(15:16:18:19) sts, patt to end.
Rep the last 2 rows once more.
Patt 32(36:40:44:48) sts, leave these sts on a holder for back
neck, patt across sts on first two holders for buttonband, dec
each cable to 2 sts. 22(24:26:28:31) sts.

Buttonband
Rib 4 rows as set.
Cast off in rib.

FRONT

Work as given for back until front measures 21(23:24:27:29)cm/
8 ¼(9:9 ½:10 ½:11 ½)in from cast on edge, ending with a
wrong side row.
Shape front neck
Next row (right side) Patt 31(36:39:44:47) sts turn and work on
these sts for first side of front neck.
Next row Patt to end.
Next row Patt to last 2 sts, k2 tog.
Rep the last 2 rows until 26(30:32:36:38) sts rem.
Cont straight until front measures same as back to shoulder,
ending at armhole edge.
Shape shoulder
Cast off 13(15:16:18:19) sts at beg of next row.
Work 1 row.
Cast off rem 13(15:16:18:19) sts.
With right side facing, slip centre 22(24:26:28:30) sts on a
holder, patt to end.
Next row Patt to end.
Next row Skpo, patt to end.
Rep the last 2 rows until 26(30:32:36:38) sts rem.
Cont straight until 6 rows less have been worked than on back
to shoulder, ending at armhole edge.
Next row Patt to end, dec each cable to 2 sts.
Leave these sts on a holder.

SLEEVES

With 3mm (US 2) needles cast on 42(42:42:50:50) sts.
1st row (right side) K2, * p2, k2; rep from * to end.
2nd row P2, * k2, p2; rep from * to end.
Rep the last 2 rows 3 times more and the 1st row again.
Inc row (wrong side) P2, * k2, m1p, p2, m1p, k2, p2; rep from * to end. 52(52:52:62:62) sts.
Change to 3.25mm (US 3) needles.
Work in patt as follows:
1st row (right side) K2, * p2, k4, p2, k2; rep from * to end.
2nd row P2, * k2, p4, k2, p2; rep from * to end.
3rd row K2, * p2, C4F, p2, k2; rep from * to end.
4th row As 2nd row.
5th row K2, * p2, k4, p2, k2; rep from * to end.
6th row As 2nd row.
These 6 rows **set** the patt.
Inc and work into patt one st at each end of the next (next:5th:5th:7th) row and every foll 4th row until there are 68(74:82:92:98) sts.
Cont straight until sleeve measures 16(19:22:25:28)cm/ 6 ¼(7 ½:8 ½:9 ¾:11)in from cast on edge, ending with a wrong side row.
Mark each end of last row with a coloured thread.
Work a further 4 rows.
Cast off in patt.

NECKBAND

Join left shoulder seam.
With right side facing, using 3mm (US 2) needles, pick up and k4(5:5:5:5) sts across row ends of button band, k0(0:0:0:1), p0(0:0:1:2), k0(0:1:2:2), p0(1:2:2:2), k1(0:0:0:0), [k2tog] 1(2:2:2:2) times, p2, k2, p2, [k2tog] twice, p2, k2, p2, [k2tog] twice, p2, k2, p2, [k2tog] 1(2:2:2:2) times, k1(0:0:0:0), p0(1:2:2:2), k0(0:1:2:2), p0(0:0:1:2), k0(0:0:0:1) across back neck sts, pick up and k14(16:17:18:19) sts evenly down left front neck, k0(0:0:1:2), p0(1:2:2:2), k2, p2, [k2tog] twice, p2, k2, p2, [k2tog] twice, p2, k2, p0(1:2:2:2), k0(0:0:1:2) across front neck sts, pick up and k11(12:13:14:15) sts evenly up right side of front neck. 73(81:89:97:105) sts.
1st, 3rd and 5th sizes only
1st row P3, [k2, p2] to last 2 sts, k2.
2nd and 4th sizes only
1st row K3, [p2, k2] to last 2 sts, p2.
This row **sets** the rib patt.
Work a further 4 rows.
Leaving last st on needle, cast off in rib.
Buttonhole band
With st on right hand needle, pick up and k4(4:4:4:3) sts across row ends of neckband, rib across sts on holder. 27(29:31:33:35) sts.
Next (buttonhole) row Rib 5, [yrn, work 2 tog, rib 7(8:9:10:11) twice, yrn, work 2 tog, rib 2.
Rib 2 rows.
Cast off in rib.

TO MAKE UP

Lap buttonhole band over button band and tack in place. Sew sleeves into armholes with row-ends above markers sewn to sts cast off at underarm. Join side and sleeve seams.
Sew on buttons.

CECILIA
COAT

From left to right: **Cecilia Coat** in Midnight (101) and Snow (124), **Cecilia Coat** in Putty Grey (121) and Storm (102) pattern on page 48

47

CECILIA COAT

SKILL LEVEL Improving

SIZES / MEASUREMENTS

To fit age	1-2	2-3	3-4	4-5	years

ACTUAL GARMENT MEASUREMENTS

Chest	70	74	79	83	cm
	27 ½	29	31	33	in
Length to	48	52	56	60	cm
shoulder	19	20 ½	22	23 ¾	in
Sleeve	21	23	25	28	cm
length	8 ¼	9	9 ¾	11	in

MATERIALS

- 14(16:17:19) 50g/1 ¾oz balls of MillaMia Naturally Soft Merino in Putty Grey (121) (M).
- Two balls in contrast colour Storm (102) (C).
- Pair each 4.50mm (US 7) and 5mm (US 8) knitting needles.
- 8 large (approx 23mm/⅞ in diameter) and 4 small (approx 18mm/¾in diameter) buttons.

TENSION / GAUGE

18 sts and 26 rows to 10cm/4in square over st st using 5mm (US 8) needles and yarn double.

HINTS AND TIPS

Using the yarn double, means that this elegant, practical winter coat will be warm and sturdy. An added benefit is that it knits up quickly working on the larger 5mm (US 8) needles. Keeping to the recommended tension ensures a neat, graceful fit. The scarf can also be used separately from the coat should you wish.

ABBREVIATIONS

See page 9.

SUGGESTED ALTERNATIVE COLOURWAYS

| Midnight 101 | Snow 124 | Plum 162 | Claret 104 | Snow 124 | Petal 122 |

NOTE

Use yarn double **throughout.**

35 (37 : 39 ½ : 41 ½) cm
13 ¾ (14 ½ : 15 ½ : 16 ½) in

21 (23 : 25 : 28) cm
8 ¼ (9 : 9 ¾ : 11) in

48 (52 : 56 : 60) cm
19 (20 ½ : 22 : 23 ¾) in

97 (107:117:127) cm / 38 (42:46:50) in

5 ½ (6 ½) cm / 2 ¼ (2 ½) in
(unstretched)

BACK

With 4.50mm (US 7) needles and M used double cast on 83(89:95:101) sts.
K 3 rows.
Change to C.
K 8 rows.
Change to 5mm (US 8) needles and M.
Beg with a k row cont in st st.
Work 8 rows.
Dec row K5, skpo, k to last 7 sts, k2 tog, k5.
Work 7 rows.
Rep the last 8 rows 8(9:10:11) times more. 65(69:73:77) sts.
Shape armholes
Cast off 4 sts at beg of next 2 rows. 57(61:65:69) sts.
Next row K2, skpo, k to last 4 sts, k2 tog, k2.
Next row P to end.
Rep the last 2 rows 2(3:3:4) times more. 51(53:57:59) sts.
Work straight until armhole measures 14(15:16:17)cm/5 ½ (6:6 ¼:6 ¾)in, ending with a wrong side row.
Shape shoulders
Cast off 6(6:7:7) sts at beg of next 2 rows and 7(7:8:8) sts at beg of foll 2 rows.
Cast off rem 25(27:27:29) sts.

LEFT FRONT

With 4.50mm (US 7) needles and M used double cast on 34(37:40:43) sts.
K 3 rows.
Change to C.
K 8 rows.
Change to 5mm (US 8) needles and M.
Beg with a k row cont in st st.
Work 8 rows.
Dec row K5, skpo, k to end.
Work 7 rows.
Rep the last 8 rows 8(9:10:11) times more. 25(27:29:31) sts.

Shape armhole
Next row Cast off 4 sts, k to end. 21(23:25:27) sts.
Next row P to end.
Next row K2, skpo, k to end.
Next row P to end.
Rep the last 2 rows 2(3:3:4) times more. 18(19:21:22) sts.
Work straight until armhole measures 9(10:10:11)cm/ 3 ½(4:4:4 ¼)in, ending with a wrong side row.
Shape neck
Next row K to last 4 sts, k2 tog, k2.
Next row P to end.
Rep the last 2 rows 4(5:5:6) times more. 13(13:15:15) sts.
Work straight until front measures same as back to shoulder, ending at armhole edge.
Shape shoulder
Cast off 6(6:7:7) sts at beg of next row.
Work 1 row.
Cast off rem 7(7:8:8) sts.

RIGHT FRONT

With 4.50mm (US 7) needles and M used double cast on 34(37:40:43) sts.
K 3 rows.
Change to C.
K 8 rows.
Change to 5mm (US 8) needles and M.
Beg with a k row cont in st st.
Work 8 rows.
Dec row K to last 7 sts, k2 tog, k5.
Work 7 rows.
Rep the last 8 rows 8(9:10:11) times more. 25(27:29:31) sts.
Work 1 row.
Shape armhole
Next row Cast off 4 sts, p to end. 21(23:25:27) sts.
Next row K to last 4 sts, k2 tog, k2.
Next row P to end.
Rep the last 2 rows 2(3:3:4) times more. 18(19:21:22) sts.

Work straight until armhole measures 9(10:10:11)cm/
3 ½(4:4:4 ¼)in, ending with a wrong side row.
Shape neck
Next row K2, skpo, k to end.
Next row P to end.
Rep the last 2 rows 4(5:5:6) times more. 13(13:15:15) sts.
Work straight until front measures same as back to shoulder,
ending at armhole edge.
Shape shoulder
Cast off 6(6:7:7) sts at beg of next row.
Work 1 row.
Cast off rem 7(7:8:8) sts.

SLEEVES

With 4.50mm (US 7) needles and M used double cast on
30(34:38:42) sts.
1st rib row K2, [p2, k2] to end.
2nd rib row P2, [k2, p2] to end.
These 2 rows form the rib.
Work 2 rows C, then 10(10:12:12) rows M.
Change to 5mm (US 8) needles.
Beg with a k row cont in st st.
Work 2(4:4:6) rows.
Inc row K3, m1, k to last 3 sts, m1, k3.
Work 3 rows.
Rep the last 4 rows 8(8:9:9) times more, and then the inc row
again. 50(54:60:64) sts.
Cont straight until sleeve measures 21(23:25:28)cm/8 ¼(9:
9 ¾: 11)in from cast on edge, ending with a p row.
Shape sleeve top
Cast off 4 sts at beg of next 2 rows. 42(46:52:56) sts.
Next row K2, skpo, k to last 4 sts, k2 tog, k2.
Next row P to end.
Rep the last 2 rows 4(5:5:6) times more. 32(34:40:42) sts.
Cast off 3 sts at beg of next 6(6:8:8) rows. 14(16:16:18) sts.
Cast off.

BUTTONBAND

With right side facing, starting at beg of neck shaping, using
4.50mm (US 7) needles and M used double, pick up and
k86(94:98:106) sts evenly down left front edge.
1st rib row P2, [k2, p2] to end.
2nd rib row K2, [p2, k2] to end.
Rep the last 2 rows 11 times more and the 1st row again.
Cast off in rib.

BUTTONHOLE BAND

With right side facing, starting at cast on edge, using
4.50mm (US 7) needles and M used double, pick up and
k86(94:98:106) sts evenly up right front edge.
1st rib row P2, [k2, p2] to end.
2nd rib row K2, [p2, k2] to end.
3rd row As 1st row.
Buttonhole row Rib 44(52:56:64), [k2 tog, yrn, rib 10] 3 times,
k2 tog, yrn, p2, k2.
Rib 17 rows.
Buttonhole row Rib 44(52:56:64), [k2 tog, yrn, rib 10] 3 times,
k2 tog, yrn, p2, k2.
Rib 3 rows.
Cast off in rib.

COLLAR

Join shoulder seams.
With right side facing, starting at beg of neck shaping,
using 4.50mm (US 7) needles and M used double, pick up
and k14(15:17:18) sts up right side of front neck, cast on
38(40:40:42) sts, pick up and k14(15:17:18) sts down left side
of front neck. 66(70:74:78) sts.
1st row K4, [p2, k2] to last 6 sts, p2, k4.
2nd row K2, [p2, k2] to end.
This patt creates a rib collar with g-st edge.
Rep the last 2 rows 5(6:7:8) times more.

Change to 5mm (US 8) needles.

Work a further 16(18:20:22) rows.

Buttonhole row K4, p2 tog, yon, rib to last 6 sts, yrn, p2 tog, k4.

Work 1 row.

Work 2 rows C, 2 rows M.

Using M cast off in rib.

POCKETS (make 2)

With 4.50mm (US 7) needles and M used double, cast on 19(20:21:22) sts.

K 1 row.

Change to C.

K 4 rows.

Change to 5mm (US 8) needles and M.

1st row K to end.

2nd row K1, p to last st, k1.

Rep the last 2 rows until pocket measures 9(9:10:10)cm/ 3 ½(3 ½:4:4)in from cast on edge, ending with a 1st row.

Next row K to end.

Next row K2, p to last 2 sts, k2.

Rep the last 2 rows once more.

Change to C.

K 2 rows.

Change to M.

K 1 row.

Cast off.

SCARF

With 4.50mm (US 7) needles and M used double cast on 18(18:22:22) sts.

1st rib row K2, [p2, k2] to end.

2nd rib row P2, [k2, p2] to end.

These 2 rows form the rib.

Work 2 rows C, then cont in M until scarf measures 95(105:115:125)cm/37 ½(41 ¼:45 ¼:49 ¼)in from cast on edge.

Work 2 rows C, then 2 rows M.

Cast off in M.

TO MAKE UP

Sew cast on edge of collar to cast off sts on back neck. Join side and sleeve seams. Sew in sleeves. Sew on pockets and catch foldover pocket top on right side.

Sew large buttons on left front button band.

Sew small buttons on neck edge for collar and to centre of each pocket top.

Block the scarf slightly stretched to make it wider and more elegant. Thread scarf through collar.

LILLEN
TOP AND BOTTOMS
LENA
BLANKET

From left to right: **Lillen Top and Bottoms** in Forget me not (120) patterns on page 56 and 60, **Lena Blanket** (on floor) in Snow (124) and Forget me not (120) pattern on page 64, **Lillen Top and Bottoms** in Petal (122) patterns on page 56 and 60

LILLEN TOP

SKILL LEVEL **Beginner**

SIZES / MEASUREMENTS

To fit age	0-3	3-6	6-12	12-18	18-24	mths

ACTUAL GARMENT MEASUREMENTS

Chest	47	52	55	58	63	cm
	18 ½	20 ½	21 ½	23	25	in
Length to shoulder	21	24	26	28	32	cm
	8 ¼	9 ½	10 ¼	11	12 ½	in
Sleeve length	13	15	17	19	22	cm
	5	6	6 ¾	7 ½	8 ¾	in

MATERIALS

- 2(3:3:4:4) 50g/1 ¾oz balls of MillaMia Naturally Soft Merino in Petal (122).
- Pair each of 3mm (US 2) and 3.25mm (US 3) knitting needles.

TENSION / GAUGE

25 sts and 34 rows to 10cm/4in square over st st using 3.25mm (US 3) needles.

HINTS AND TIPS

A great introduction to moss (seed) stitch for beginners, with this stitch being used on the hem and borders. The wide neck makes it easy to get on and off babies and small children.

ABBREVIATIONS

See page 9.

SUGGESTED ALTERNATIVE COLOURWAYS

Forget me not 120	Putty Grey 121	Daisy Yellow 142	Midnight 101	Scarlet 140

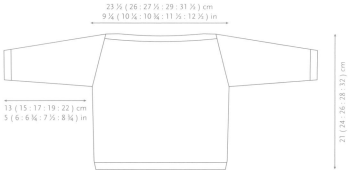

23 ½ (26 : 27 ½ : 29 : 31 ½) cm
9 ¼ (10 ¼ : 10 ¾ : 11 ½ : 12 ½) in

13 (15 : 17 : 19 : 22) cm
5 (6 : 6 ¾ : 7 ½ : 8 ¾) in

21 (24 : 26 : 28 : 32) cm
8 ¼ (9 ½ : 10 ¼ : 11 : 12 ½) in

BACK and FRONT (alike)

With 3mm (US 2) needles cast on 61(67:71:75:81) sts.
Moss st row K1, * p1, k1; rep from * to end.
This row forms moss st.
Rep the last row 5 times more.
Change to 3.25mm (US 3) needles.
Beg with a k row, work in st st until back measures
11(13:14:15:18)cm/4 ½(5 ¼:5 ½:6:7)in from cast on edge,
ending with a p row.
Mark each end of last row with a coloured thread.
Shape armholes
Dec row K3, skpo, k to last 5 sts, k2 tog, k3.
Work 7 rows.
Rep the last 8 rows 2(2:3:3:4) times more, and then the dec
row again. 53(59:61:65:69) sts.
Work 5(9:5:7:3) rows.
Change to 3mm (US 2) needles.
Work 4 rows moss st.
Cast off in moss st.

SLEEVES

With 3mm (US 2) needles cast on 29(29:33:35:37) sts.
Moss st row P1, * k1, p1; rep from * to end.
This row forms moss st.
Rep the last row 5 times more.
Change to 3.25mm (US 3) needles.
Beg with a k row, work in st st.
Work 2 rows.
Inc row K3, m1, k to last 3 sts, m1, k3.
Work 3 rows.
Rep the last 4 rows 7(9:10:12:15) times more, and then the inc
row again. 47(51:57:63:71) sts.
Cont straight until sleeve measures 13(15:17:19:22)cm/
5(6:6 ¾:7 ½:8 ¾)in from cast on edge, ending with a p row.
Mark each end of last row with a coloured thread.
Shape top
Cast off 3 sts at beg of next 8(8:10:12:14) rows.
23(27:27:27:29) sts.
Cast off.

TO MAKE UP

Leaving centre 43(45:47:49:51) sts open for neck, join shoulder
seams. 5(7:7:8:9) sts to join on each side of centre opening.
Matching coloured threads and with centre of cast off edge of
sleeve to shoulder, sew on sleeves. Join side and sleeve seams.

LILLEN BOTTOMS

SKILL LEVEL **Beginner**

SIZES / MEASUREMENTS

To fit age	0-3	3-6	6-12	12-18	18-24	mths

ACTUAL GARMENT MEASUREMENTS

Over	41	46	51	56	61	cm
nappy	16	18	20	22	24	in
Length	29	32	35	39	43	cm
	11 ½	12 ½	13 ¾	15 ¼	17	in

MATERIALS

- 2(2:3:3:4) 50g/1 ¾oz balls of MillaMia Naturally Soft Merino in Forget me not (120).
- Pair each 3mm (US 2) and 3.25mm (US 3) knitting needles.
- Optional: Waist length of elastic.

TENSION / GAUGE

25 sts and 34 rows to 10cm/4in square over st st using 3.25mm (US 3) needles.

HINTS AND TIPS

Like the Lillen Top, a great introduction to moss (seed) stitch for beginner knitters, with attractive moss stitch hems. Block the legs wide at the base to achieve the fun, flared leg.

ABBREVIATIONS

See page 9.

SUGGESTED ALTERNATIVE COLOURWAYS

Petal	Putty Grey	Daisy Yellow	Midnight	Lilac Blossom
122	121	142	101	123

20 ½ (23 : 25 ½ : 28 : 30 ½) cm
8 (9 : 10 : 11 : 12) in

29 (32 : 35 : 39 : 43) cm
11 ½ (12 ½ : 13 ¾ : 15 ¼ : 17) in

LEGS (make 2)

Starting at waistband, with 3mm (US 2) needles cast on
54(60:66:72:78) sts.

Rib row [K1, p1] to end.

Work a further 11(11:13:13:15) rows in rib.

Change to 3.25mm (US 3) needles.

Beg with a k row, cont in st st until work measures
14(15:17:18:20)cm/5 ½(6:6 ¾:7:8)in from cast on edge, ending
with a p row.

Shape crotch

Inc row K2, m1, k to last 2 sts, m1, k2.

Next row P to end.

Rep the last 2 rows 2(2:3:3:4) times more. 60(66:74:80:88) sts.

Cast on 3(3:3:4:4) sts at beg of next 2 rows. 66(72:80:88:96) sts.

Shape for leg

Work 2 rows.

Next row K2, skpo, k to last 4 sts, k2 tog, k2.

Next row P to end.

Rep the last 2 rows 2(3:4:5:6) times more. 60(64:70:76:82) sts.

Cont straight until work measures 27(30:33:37:41)cm/10 ¾
(11 ¾:13:14 ½:16 ¼)in from cast on edge, ending with a p row.

Change to 3mm (US 2) needles.

1st moss st row [K1, p1] to end.

2nd moss st row [P1, k1] to end.

Rep the last 2 rows 4 times more.

Cast off in moss st.

MAKE UP

Join inner leg seams. Join centre front and back seam.
Optional: Join elastic into a ring. Work a herringbone casing
over rib at waist, enclosing elastic.

LENA BLANKET

SKILL LEVEL **Beginner / Improving**

SIZES / MEASUREMENTS

To fit age   One size

ACTUAL MEASUREMENTS

Length	77	cm
	30 ½	in
Width	62 ½	cm
	24 ½	in

MATERIALS

- Seven 50g/1 ¾oz balls of MillaMia Naturally Soft Merino in Snow (124) (M).
- Two balls contrast colour in Forget me not (120) (C).
- Pair of 3.25mm (US 3) knitting needles.

TENSION / GAUGE

25 sts and 34 rows to 10cm/4in over st st using 3.25mm (US 3) needles.
26 sts and 44 rows to 10cm/4in square over moss (seed) st using 3.25mm (US 3) needles.

HINTS AND TIPS

This blanket is beautiful and timeless. Vary the colour border for a completely different look, for instance teaming a bright fuchsia border with a midnight navy blanket. Easy to knit, with a combination of stocking and moss (seed) stitch and a simple colour border.

ABBREVIATIONS

See page 9.

SUGGESTED ALTERNATIVE COLOURWAYS

| Lilac Blossom 123 | Storm 102 | Midnight 101 | Fuchsia 143 | Plum 162 | Putty Grey 121 |

TO MAKE

With 3.25mm (US 3) needles and M cast on 163 sts.
1st row *K1, p1; rep from * to last st, k1.
This row forms the moss st patt. Cont in patt until the 34th row has been worked.
35th row (right side) [K1, p1] 10 times in M, change to C, twisting on the wrong side, k123, twisting on wrong side join in another ball of M and [p1, k1] 10 times.
36th row [K1, p1] 10 times in M, twisting on the wrong side change to C and p123, twisting on wrong side change to M and [p1, k1] 10 times.
Rep the last 2 rows 6 times more.
49th row [K1, p1] 10 times in M, with C k10, join in another

ball of M k103, join in another ball of C k10, with M [p1, k1] 10 times.
50th row [K1, p1] 10 times in M, with C p10, with M p103, with C p10, with M [p1, k1] 10 times.
Rep the last 2 rows until blanket measures 66cm/26in from cast on edge.
Rep 35th and 36th row, 7 times more.
Cut off C. Cont in M.
Rep 35th row using M only.
Rep 1st row 34 times.
Cast off.
Sew in ends.

62 ½ cm / 24 ½ in

77 cm / 30 ½ in

VIKTORIA
CARDIGAN
VIKTOR
BLAZER

From left to right: **Viktoria Cardigan** in Claret (104) and Plum (162) and **Viktoria Cardigan** in Snow (124) and Midnight (101) pattern on page 72, **Viktor Blazer** in Midnight (101) and Snow (124) pattern on page 68

VIKTOR BLAZER

SKILL LEVEL **Experienced**

SIZES / MEASUREMENTS

To fit age	2-3	3-4	4-5	years

ACTUAL GARMENT MEASUREMENTS

Chest	68	73	78	cm
	27	29	31	in
Length to shoulder	36	40	44	cm
	14 ¼	15 ¾	17 ¼	in
Sleeve length	24	27	30	cm
	9 ½	10 ½	11 ¾	in

MATERIALS

- 8(9:10) 50g/1 ¾oz balls of MillaMia Naturally Soft Merino in Midnight (101) (M).
- One ball contrast colour in Snow (124) (C).
- Pair each of 3mm (US 2) and 3.25mm (US 3) knitting needles.
- 4 white buttons (approx 15mm/⅝ in diameter).

TENSION / GAUGE

26 sts and 44 rows to 10cm/4in square over moss (seed) st using 3.25mm (US 3) needles.

HINTS AND TIPS

A stylish boy's blazer that has been designed to take advantage of the reversible qualities of moss (seed) stitch. This has enabled the collar to be knitted as part of the main body rather than a separate piece to be added. Pressing the collar in place with an iron will help it to hold its shape.

ABBREVIATIONS

See page 9.

SUGGESTED ALTERNATIVE COLOURWAYS

Claret	Storm	Fawn	Scarlet	Seaside	Fawn
104	102	160	140	161	160

34 (36 ½ : 39) cm
13 ½ (14 ½ : 15 ½) in

36 (40 : 44) cm
14 ¼ (15 ¾ : 17 ¼) in

24 (27 : 30) cm
9 ½ (10 ½ : 11 ¾) in

BACK

With 3.25mm (US 3) needles and C cast on 91(97:103) sts.
Moss st row K1, [p1, k1] to end.
Rep the last row 9 times more.
Cut off C.
Join on M.
Cont in moss st until back measures 24(27:30)cm/9 ½(10 ½:
11 ¾)in from cast on edge, ending with a wrong side row.
Shape armholes
Cast off 4 sts at beg of next 2 rows.
Dec one st at each end of the next and 3 foll right side rows.
75(81:87) sts.
Cont straight until back measures 36(40:44)cm/14 ¼(15 ¾:
17 ¼)in from cast on edge, ending with a wrong side row.
Shape shoulders
Cast off 11(12:13) sts at beg of next 4 rows.
Cast off rem 31(33:35) sts.

RIGHT FRONT

With 3.25mm (US 3) needles and C cast on 49(53:57) sts.
Moss st row P1, [k1, p1] to end.
Rep the last row 9 times more.
Next row Moss st 6C, join in M, using M moss st to end.
Next row Using M moss st to last 6 sts, twist yarns on wrong
side, moss st 6C.
These 2 rows form the moss st body with contrast edging.
Cont in patt until front measures 21(24:27)cm/8 ¼(9 ½:10 ½)in
from cast on edge.
Now twist yarns on right side of work – this will become the
wrong side of collar.
Cont in patt until front measures 24(27:30)cm/9 ½(10 ½:11 ¾)in
from cast on edge, ending with a right side row.
Shape armhole
Cast off 4 sts at beg of next row.
Dec one st at armhole edge on the next and 3 foll right side
rows. 41(45:49) sts.

Cont straight until front measures 28(31:34)cm/11(12 ¼:13 ¼)in
from cast on edge, ending with a wrong side row.
Shape neck
Next row Moss st 13(14:15) C, leave these sts on a holder,
using M moss st to end.
Dec one st at neck edge on every right side row until 22(24:26)
sts rem.
Work straight until front matches the same as back to
shoulder, ending at side edge.
Shape shoulder
Cast off 11(12:13) sts at beg of next row.
Work 1 row.
Cast off rem 11(12:13) sts.
Place markers for 4 buttons. The first on the 12th row from
cast on edge, the 4th 5cm/2in below armhole shaping and the
rem two spaced evenly between.

LEFT FRONT

With 3.25mm (US 3) needles and C cast on 49(53:57) sts.
Moss st row P1, [k1, p1] to end.
Rep the last row 9 times more.
Cut off C.
Join on M.
Next row Using M moss st to last 6 sts, join in C, moss st 6C.
Buttonhole row Using C, p1, k1, p2 tog, yrn, p1, k1, twist yarns
on wrong side, using M moss st to end.
Next row Using M moss st to last 6 sts, moss st 6C.
Next row Moss st 6C, twist yarns on wrong side, using M
moss st to end.
These 2 rows form the moss st body with contrast edging.
Working rem 3 buttonholes to match markers on right front,
cont in patt until front measures 21(24:27)cm/8 ¼(9 ½:10 ½)in
from cast on edge.
Now twist yarns on right side of work – this will become the
wrong side of collar.
Cont in patt until front measures 24(27:30)cm/9 ½(10 ½:11 ¾)in
from cast on edge, ending with a wrong side row.

Shape armhole

Cast off 4 sts at beg of next row.

Work 1 row.

Dec one st at armhole edge on the next and 3 foll right side rows. 41(45:49) sts.

Cont straight until front measures 28(31:34)cm/11(12 ¼:13 ¼)in from cast on edge, ending with a wrong side row.

Shape neck

Next row Patt to last 13(14:15) sts, leave these sts on a holder.

Dec one st at neck edge on every right side row until 22(24:26) sts rem.

Work straight until front matches the same as back to shoulder, ending at side edge.

Shape shoulder

Cast off 11(12:13) sts at beg of next row.

Work 1 row.

Cast off rem 11(12:13) sts.

SLEEVES

With 3.25mm (US 3) needles and C cast on 35(39:41) sts.

Moss st row K1, [p1, k1] to end.

Rep the last row 9 times more.

Cut off C.

Join on M.

Work a further 6 rows.

Inc and work into moss st one st at each end of the next row and every foll 6th row until there are 61(67:73) sts.

Cont straight until sleeve measures 24(27:30)cm/ 9 ½(10 ½: 11 ¾)in from cast on edge, ending with a wrong side row.

Shape sleeve top

Cast off 4 sts at beg of next 2 rows.

Dec one st at each end of the next and 7(7:8) foll right side rows then on every foll 4th row until 31(35:39) sts rem.

Cast off 2 sts at beg of next 8 rows.

Cast off.

COLLAR

Join shoulder seams.

With right side facing using 3mm (US 2) needles, place 13(14:15) sts from right front holder on a needle, using M, pick up and p20(22:24) sts up right side of front neck, pick up and k31(33:35) sts across back neck, pick up and p20(22:24) sts down right side of front neck, using C, moss st 13(14:15) sts from left front holder. 97(105:113) sts.

Next row (right side) Using C moss st 13(14:15) sts, using M moss st 71(77:83) sts using C moss st 13(14:15) sts.

This row forms the moss st.

Next 2 rows Patt to last 33(36:39) sts, turn.

Next 2 rows Patt to last 29(31:33) sts, turn.

Next 2 rows Patt to last 25(26:27) sts, turn.

Next 2 rows Patt to last 20(21:22) sts, turn.

Next 2 rows Patt to last 15(16:17) sts, turn.

Next row Patt to end.

Twisting yarns on wrong side when changing colour, work a further 5 rows across all sts.

Cast off 7(8:9) sts at beg of next 2 rows.

Change to 3.25mm (US 3) needles.

Work a further 3cm/1 ¼in as set, ending with a wrong side row.

Cont in C only for a further 8 rows.

Cast off.

TO MAKE UP

Join side and sleeve seams. Sew in sleeves. Sew on buttons.

VIKTORIA CARDIGAN

SKILL LEVEL **Beginner / Improving**

SIZES / MEASUREMENTS

To fit age	0-3	3-6	6-12	12-24	24-36	36-48	mths

ACTUAL GARMENT MEASUREMENTS

Chest	48	52	56	58	64	68	cm
	19	20 ½	22	23	25	26 ½	in
Length to	23	25	28	31	34	38	cm
shoulder	9	10	11	12 ¼	13 ¼	15	in
Sleeve	13	15	17	19	22	25	cm
length	5	6	6 ¾	7 ½	8 ¾	9 ¾	in

MATERIALS

- 2(3:3:4:4:5) 50g/1 ¾oz balls of MillaMia Naturally Soft Merino in Snow (124) (M).
- One ball contrast colour in Midnight (101) (C).
- Pair each of 3mm (US 2) and 3.25mm (US 3) knitting needles.
- One button (approx 18mm/¾in diameter).

TENSION / GAUGE

25 sts and 34 rows to 10cm/4in square over st st using 3.25mm(US 3) needles.

HINTS AND TIPS

When changing the colour of yarn to form the garter stitch trim, take care to twist the two colours around each other once on the wrong side to prevent a gap from forming at the colour change join.

ABBREVIATIONS

See page 9.

SUGGESTED ALTERNATIVE COLOURWAYS

Claret	Plum		Midnight	Grass		Fuchsia	Storm
104	162		101	141		143	102

24 (26 : 28 : 29 : 32 : 34) cm
9 ½ (10 ¼ : 11 : 11 ½ : 12 ½ : 13 ¼) in

23 (25 : 28 : 31 : 34 : 38) cm
9 (10 : 11 : 12 ¼ : 13 ¼ : 15) in

13 (15 : 17 : 19 : 22 : 25) cm
5 (6 : 6 ¾ : 7 ½ : 8 ¾ : 9 ¾) in

BACK

With 3mm (US 2) needles and C cast on 61(67:71:75:81:87) sts.
K7(7:7:9:9:9) rows. This forms g-st trim.
Break off C.
Join on M.
Change to 3.25mm (US 3) needles.
Beg with a k row, work in st st until back measures
13(14:16:18:20:23)cm/5(5 ½:6 ¼:7:8:9)in from cast on edge,
ending with a p row.
Shape armholes
Cast off 4 sts at beg of next 2 rows. 53(59:63:67:73:79) sts.
Next row K2, skpo, k to last 4 sts, k2 tog, k2.
Next row P to end.
Rep the last 2 rows 1(2:2:2:3:4) times. 49(53:57:61:65:69) sts.
Cont straight until back measures 23(25:28:31:34:38)cm/
9(10:11:12 ¼:13 ¼:15)in from cast on edge, ending with
a p row.
Shape shoulders
Cast off 11(12:13:14:15:16) sts at beg of next 2 rows.
Leave rem 27(29:31:33:35:37) sts on a holder.

LEFT FRONT

With 3mm (US 2) needles and C cast on 31(34:36:38:41:44) sts.
K7(7:7:9:9:9) rows. This forms g-st trim.
Change to 3.25mm (US 3) needles.
Break off C.
Join on M.
Next row (right side) With M, k to last 6 sts, join on C, k6C.
Next row K6C, with M p to end.
These 2 rows form the st st with g-st border.
Work straight until front measures 13(14:16:18:20:23)cm/5(5 ½:
6 ¼:7:8:9)in from cast on edge, ending with a wrong side row.
Shape armhole
Cast off 4 sts at beg of next row. 27(30:32:34:37:40) sts.
Next row Patt to end.
Next row K2, skpo, patt to end.

Rep the last 2 rows 1(2:2:2:3:4) times. 25(27:29:31:33:35) sts.
Work straight until front measures 19(21:23:26:28:32)cm/
7 ½(8 ¼:9:10 ¼:11:12 ½)in from cast on edge, ending with a
wrong side row.
Shape neck
Next row K to last 6(7:8:9:10:11) sts, leave these sts on a holder.
Next row P to end.
Next row K to last 4 sts, k2 tog, k2.
Next row P2, p2 tog, p to end.
Rep the last 2 rows until 11(12:13:14:15:16) sts rem.
Cont straight until front measures same as back to shoulder,
ending at armhole edge.
Shape shoulder
Cast off.

RIGHT FRONT

With 3mm (US 2) needles and C cast on 31(34:36:38:41:44) sts.
K7(7:7:9:9:9) rows.
Change to 3.25mm (US 3) needles.
Next row (right side) K6C, join on M k to end.
Next row With M, p to last 6 sts, k6C.
These 2 rows form the st st with g-st border.
Work straight until front measures 13(14:16:18:20:23)cm/5(5 ½:
6 ¼:7:8:9)in from cast on edge, ending with a right side row.
Shape armhole
Cast off 4 sts at beg of next row. 27(30:32:34:37:40) sts.
Next row Patt to last 4 sts, k2 tog, k2.
Next row Patt to end.
Rep the last 2 rows 1(2:2:2:3:4) times. 25(27:29:31:33:35) sts.
Work straight until front measures 19(21:23:26:28:32)cm/
7 ½(8 ¼:9:10 ¼:11:12 ½)in from cast on edge, ending with a
wrong side row.
Shape neck
Next row With C, cast on 4 sts, k these 4 sts, then
k6(7:8:9:10:11)C, leave these 10(11:12:13:14:15) sts on a
holder, then with M, k to end.
Next row P to end.

Next row K2, skpo, k to end.
Next row P to last 4 sts, p2 tog tbl, p2.
Rep the last 2 rows until 11(12:13:14:15:16) sts rem.
Cont straight until front measures same as back to shoulder, ending at armhole edge.
Shape shoulder
Cast off.

SLEEVES

With 3mm (US 2) needles and C cast on 27(27:31:35:37:41) sts.
K7(7:7:9:9:9) rows.
Break off C.
Join on M.
Change to 3.25mm (US 3) needles.
Beg with a k row, work in st st.
Work 2 rows.
Inc row K3, m1, k to last 3 sts, m1, k3.
Work 3 rows.
Rep the last 4 rows 7(9:10:11:13:14) times more, and then the inc row again. 45(49:55:61:67:73) sts.
Cont straight until sleeve measures 13(15:17:19:22:25)cm/
5(6:6 ¾:7 ½: 8 ¾:9 ¾)in from cast on edge, ending with a p row.
Shape sleeve top
Cast off 4 sts at beg of next 2 rows. 37(41:47:53:59:65) sts.
Next row K2, skpo, k to last 4 sts, k2 tog, k2.
Next row P to end.
Rep the last 2 rows 9(10:10:10:11:12) times.
17(19:25:31:35:39) sts.
Cast off 2 sts at beg of next 4(4:6:6:8:8) rows.
Cast off.

NECKBAND

Join shoulder seams.
With right side facing and 3mm (US 2) needles and using C, slip 10(11:12:13:14:15) sts from right front neck holder onto a needle, pick up and k16(16:17:17:18:18) sts up right front neck, k27(29:31:33:35:37) sts from back neck holder, pick up and k16(16:17:17:18:18) sts down left front neck, k6(7:8:9:10:11) sts from left front holder. 75(79:85:89:95:99) sts.
Next row Cast on 4 sts, k to end.
K 4 rows.
Next row (buttonhole row) K2, k2 tog, y2rn (see note in italics below), skpo, k to end.
K 5 rows.
Cast off.
The y2rn (US yo2) results in a bigger buttonhole than you would achieve with a yrn (US yo). Simply wrap the yarn two times around your needle rather than once as with a single yrn (US yo). On the following row work into each loop separately, working k1, k1 tbl.

TO MAKE UP

Join side and sleeve seams. Sew in sleeves. Sew on button.

KRISTINA
PONCHO
ALEX
PONCHO
ULLI
HAT AND
SCARF

From left to right: **Kristina Poncho** in Snow
(124) pattern on page 78, **Alex Poncho** in
Fawn (160) pattern on page 82, **Ulli Hat
and Scarf** in Seaside (161) and Fawn (160)
patterns on page 86

KRISTINA PONCHO

SKILL LEVEL Experienced

SIZES / MEASUREMENTS

To fit age	2-3	3-4	4-5	years

ACTUAL GARMENT MEASUREMENTS

Width at	112	122	132	cm
lower edge	44	48	52	in
Length to	33	37	41	cm
shoulder	13	14 ½	16 ¼	in

MATERIALS

- 9(10:11) 50g/1 ¾oz balls MillaMia Naturally Soft Merino in Snow (124).
- Pair each 4.50mm (US 7) and 5mm (US 8) needles.
- Cable needle.
- 5 toggles.

TENSION / GAUGE

18 sts and 26 rows to 10cm/4in square over st st using 5mm (US 8) needles and yarn double.
20 sts and 32 rows to 10cm/4in square over rib patt using 5mm(US 8) needles and yarn double.

HINTS AND TIPS

This poncho is actually very simple to construct. Made from just two flat pieces of knitting sewn together at the back seam. The neck and button band are then picked up and knitted. As with the other items knitted using the yarn double in this book, it is a really substantial and thick garment that will keep your child nice and warm.

ABBREVIATIONS

C4B – cable 4 back, slip next 2 sts onto cable needle and leave at back of work, k2, then k2 from cable needle.
C4F – cable 4 front, slip next 2 sts onto cable needle and leave at front of work, k2, then k2 from cable needle.
See also page 9.

SUGGESTED ALTERNATIVE COLOURWAYS

Putty Grey	Claret	Fawn
121	104	160

NOTE

Use yarn double **throughout.**

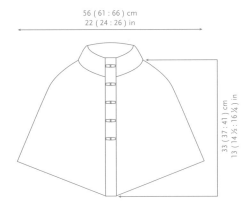

56 (61 : 66) cm
22 (24 : 26) in

33 (37 : 41) cm
13 (14 ½ : 16 ¼) in

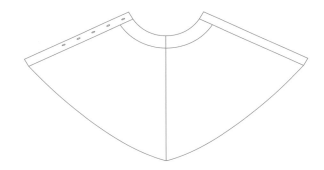

MAKE 2 PIECES (both alike)

With 5mm (US 8) needles and yarn double cast on 4 sts.
1st row K to end.
2nd row K to end.
3rd row Cast on 4 sts, k8.
4th row K4, p4.
5th row Cast on 4 sts, p4, k8.
6th row K4, p to end.
7th row Cast on 4 sts, k4, p4, k8.
8th row K4, p to end.
9th row Cast on 4 sts, k4, C4F, p4, k8.
10th row K4, p to end.
11th row Cast on 4 sts, p4, k8, p4, k8.
12th row K4, p to end.
13th row Cast on 4 sts, k4, p4, C4B, C4F, p4, k8.
14th row K4, p to end.
15th row Cast on 4 sts, p4, k4, p4, k8, p4, k8.
16th row K4, p to end.
17th row Cast on 4 sts, [k4, p4] twice, C4B, C4F, p4, k8.
18th row K4, p to end.
19th row Cast on 4 sts, k8, p4, k4, p4, k8, p4, k8.
20th row K4, p to end.
21st row Cast on 4 sts, p4, C4B, C4F, p4, k4, p4, C4B, C4F, p4, k8.
22nd row K4, p to end. 44 sts.
23rd row Cast on 4 sts, k4, p4, k8, p4, k4, p4, k8, p4, k8.
24th row K4, p to end. 48 sts.
These 24 rows set the position for the two 8 stitch cable panels
and establish the st st and g-st rib.
Cast on and work into rib patt 4 sts at beg of next and 4(6:8)
foll right side rows. 68(76:84) sts.
Work 6 rows, ending with a right side row.
Next 2 rows K4, patt 52(60:68) sts, turn, patt to end.
Rep the last 8 rows 12(13:14) times.
Work 5 rows across all sts, ending with a wrong side row.
Cast off 4 sts at beg of next and 15(17:19) foll right side rows.
Work 1 row.
Cast off rem 4 sts.

NECKBAND

Join back seam.
With right side facing, using 4.50mm (US 7) needles and yarn
double, pick up and k 68(76:84) sts evenly round neck edge.
1st row P3, [k2, p2] to last 5 sts, k2, p3.
2nd row K3, [p2, k2] to last 5 sts, p2, k3.
Rep the last 2 rows 8 times more and the 1st row again.
Cast off in rib.

BUTTONBAND

With 4.50mm (US 7) needles and yarn double pick up and
k82(90:98) sts evenly down left front edge.
1st row P2, [k2, p2] to end.
2nd row K2, [p2, k2] to end.
Rep the last 2 rows 4 times more and the 1st row again.
Cast off in rib.

BUTTONHOLE BAND

With 4.50mm (US 7) needles and yarn double pick up and k82(90:98) sts evenly down right front edge.
1st row P2, [k2, p2] to end.
2nd row K2, [p2, k2] to end.
Rep the last 2 rows once more.
Buttonhole row Rib 5, [p2 tog, y2rn (see note in italics below), p2 tog tbl, rib 8] 4 times, p2 tog, y2rn, p2 tog tbl, rib to end.
Next row Rib to end, working twice into y2rn.
Rib 5 rows.
Cast off in rib.
The y2rn (US yo2) results in a bigger buttonhole than you would achieve with a yrn (US yo). Simply wrap the yarn two times around your needle rather than once as with a single yrn (US yo).
On the following row work into each loop separately, working tbl through 2nd loop.

TO COMPLETE

Sew on toggles.

ALEX PONCHO

SKILL LEVEL **Improving / Experienced**

SIZES / MEASUREMENTS

To fit age	2-3	3-4	5-6	years

ACTUAL GARMENT MEASUREMENTS

Wrist to	64	72	80 ½	cm
wrist	25 ¼	28 ½	31 ½	in
Length to	36	46	56	cm
shoulder	14 ¼	18	22	in

MATERIALS

- 18(20:22) 50g/1 ¾oz balls MillaMia Naturally Soft Merino in Fawn (160).
- Pair 4.50mm (US 7) needles.
- Circular 4.50mm (US 7) needle and circular 5mm (US 8) needle.
- Cable needle.

TENSION / GAUGE

18 sts and 26 rows to 10cm/4in square over st st using 5mm (US 8) needles and yarn double.

24 sts and 32 rows to 10cm/4in square over patt slightly stretched using 5mm (US 8) needles and yarn double.

HINTS AND TIPS

As this poncho is knitted using the yarn double it is a really substantial and thick garment that will keep your child nice and warm.

ABBREVIATIONS

C4B – cable 4 back, slip next 2 sts onto cable needle and leave at back of work, k2, then k2 from cable needle.

See also page 9.

SUGGESTED ALTERNATIVE COLOURWAYS

Putty Grey	Moss	Snow
121	103	124

NOTE

Use yarn double **throughout**.

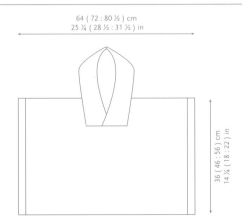

64 (72 : 80 ½) cm
25 ¼ (28 ½ : 31 ½) in

36 (46 : 56) cm
14 ¼ (18 : 22) in

BACK

With 4.50mm (US 7) circular needle and yarn double cast on 130(148:166) sts.
1st row P1, [k2, p2, k3, p2] to last 3 sts, k2, p1.
2nd row K1, [p2, k2, p3, k2] to last 3 sts, p2, k1.
Rep the last 2 rows twice more and the 1st row again.
Inc row K1, [p2, k2, p2, m1, p1, k2] to last 3 sts, p2, k1.
144(164:184) sts.
Change to 5mm (US 8) circular needle.
1st row (right side) P1, [k2, p2, k4, p2] to last 3 sts, k2, p1.
2nd row K1, [p2, k2, p4, k2] to last 3 sts, p2, k1.
3rd row P1, [k2, p2, C4B, p2] to last 3 sts, k2, p1.
4th row K1, [p2, k2, p4, k2] to last 3 sts, p2, k1.
These 4 rows form the patt.
Cont in patt until back measures 36(46:56)cm/14 ¼(18:22)in from cast on edge, ending with a wrong side row.
Shape shoulders
Cast off 54(62:70) sts at beg of next 2 rows.
Cast off rem 36(40:44) sts.

FRONT

Work as given for back until front measures 24(32:40)cm/9 ½(12 ½:15 ¾)in from cast on edge, ending with a wrong side row.
Shape neck
Next row Patt 62(72:82) sts, turn and work on these sts for first side of neck.
Cont straight until front measures the same as back to shoulder shaping, ending at side edge.
Next row Cast off 54(62:70) sts, patt to end.
Leave rem 8(10:12) sts on a holder.
With right side facing, cast off centre 20 sts, patt to end.
Complete to match first side.

SIDE BORDERS (Work 4)

With right side facing using 4.50mm (US 7) needles and yarn double pick up and k74(86:98) sts along row ends of each side of back and front.
1st row P2, * k2, p2; rep from * to end.
2nd row K2, * p2, k2; rep from * to end.
Rep the last 2 rows once more and the 1st row again.
Cast off in rib.

HOOD

Join shoulder and border seams.
With right side facing, using 4.50mm (US 7) needles and yarn double, k across 8(10:12) sts on right front neck holder, cast on 52(56:60) sts, k across 8(10:12) sts on left front neck holder. 68(76:84) sts.
Next row P3, * k2, p2; rep from * to last 5 sts, k2, p3.
Next row K3, * p2, k2; rep from * to last 5 sts, p2, k3.
Rep the last 2 rows until hood measures 19(20:21)cm/7 ½(8:8 ¼)in, ending with a wrong side row.
Shape top
Next row Patt 34(38:42) sts, turn and work on these sts.
Cast off 6 sts at beg of next and 4 foll alt rows.
Work 1 row.
Cast off rem 4(8:12) sts.
Rejoin yarn to rem sts, complete to match first side.

RIGHT FRONT BORDER (OF HOOD)

With right side facing using 4.50mm (US 7) needles and yarn double pick up and k74(82:90) sts along right front edge and right side of hood.

1st row P2, * k2, p2; rep from * to end.
2nd row K2, * p2, k2; rep from * to end.
Rep the last 2 rows 8 times, and the 1st row again.
Cast off in rib.

LEFT FRONT BORDER (OF HOOD)

With right side facing using 4.50mm (US 7) needles and yarn double pick up and k74(82:90) sts along left side of hood and left front edge.

1st row P2, * k2, p2; rep from * to end.
2nd row K2, * p2, k2; rep from * to end.
Rep the last 2 rows 8 times, and the 1st row again.
Cast off in rib.

MAKE UP

With right sides together, fold hood in half and sew shaped edge and borders. Sew cast on edge of hood to cast off sts on back neck. Lap right edge over left, and sew to cast off edge at centre front.

ULLI HAT AND SCARF

SKILL LEVEL Beginner / Improving

SIZES / MEASUREMENTS

To fit age   Toddler, one size,

ACTUAL MEASUREMENTS SCARF

Length   108   cm
              42 ½   in

Width   17   cm
              6 ¾   in

MATERIALS

- Two 50g/1 ¾oz balls of MillaMia Naturally Soft Merino in Seaside (161) (M) for hat.
- One ball contrast colour in Fawn (160) (C) for hat.
- Five 50g/1 ¾oz balls of MillaMia Naturally Soft Merino in Seaside (161) (M) for scarf.
- One ball contrast colour in Fawn (160) (C) for scarf.
- If knitting both the scarf and hat, one ball of contrast colour (C) will be enough for both patterns.
- Pair 5mm (US 8) knitting needles.
- Cable needle.

TENSION / GAUGE

28 sts and 24 rows to 10cm/4in square over single rib patt using 5mm (US 8) needles and yarn double.

HINTS AND TIPS

Knit this lovely chunky Ulli Hat and Scarf combination – a good introduction to simple cable work and refreshingly quick as you use the yarn double throughout. As you are knitting with two strands of yarn held together, but may only have one ball of yarn, simply wind off half this single ball into a separate ball before you start using it. Then weigh the two balls to make sure they are about the same size – half of a 50g/1 ¾oz ball weighs 25g/⅞oz.

ABBREVIATIONS

C8F – cable 8 front, slip next 4 sts onto cable needle and hold at front of work, k4, then k4 from cable needle.
Also see page 9.

SUGGESTED ALTERNATIVE COLOURWAYS

Midnight   Snow
101   124

Plum   Claret
162   104

NOTE

Use yarn double **throughout.**

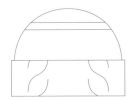

108 cm / 42 ½ in

HAT

With 5mm (US 8) needles and M used double cast on 95 sts.
1st row [K1, p1] 3 times, *k8, p1, [k1, p1] 5 times**, rep from * to ** 3 times more, k8, p1, [k1, p1] twice.
2nd row [K1, p1] twice, k1, *p8, k1, [p1, k1] 5 times**, rep from * to ** 3 times more, p8, [k1, p1] 3 times.
Rep these 2 rows twice more.
7th row [K1, p1] 3 times, *C8F, p1, [k1, p1] 5 times**, rep from * to ** 3 times more, C8F, p1, [k1, p1] twice.
8th row As 2nd row.
Rep the 1st and 2nd rows 4 times more.
17th row [K2, p2] to last 3 sts, k2, inc in last st. 96 sts.
Cont working in double rib on these 96 sts until the hat measures 15cm/6in from cast on edge.
With C, work 3 rows in double rib.
Cont in M, work 3 rows in double rib.
Shape top
1st row *K2, p2 tog; rep from * to end.
2nd row *K1, p2; rep from * to end.
3rd row *K2, p1; rep from * to end.
4th row *K1, p2; rep from * to end.
5th row *K2 tog, p1; rep from * to end.
6th row *K1, p1; rep from * to end.
7th row *K1, p3 tog; rep from * to end.
8th row *P1, p2 tog; rep from * to end.
Break yarn, thread end through rem 16 sts, pull up and secure.

MAKE UP

Join seam, reversing seam on last 6cm/2 ½in.

SCARF

With 5mm (US 8) needles and M used double cast on 47 sts.
1st row (right side) [K1, p1] 6 times, k8, p1, [k1, p1] 3 times, k8, [p1, k1] 6 times.
2nd row [P1, k1] 6 times, p8, k1, [p1, k1] 3 times, p8, [k1, p1] 6 times.
3rd row As 1st row.
4th row As 2nd row.
5th row [K1, p1] 6 times, C8F, p1, [k1, p1] 3 times, C8F, [p1, k1] 6 times.
6th row As 2nd row.
7th row As 1st row.
8th row As 2nd row.
9th row As 1st row.
10th row As 2nd row.
These 10 rows form the cable patt. Rep them 3 times more.
Next row [K1, p1] to last st, k1.
Next row [P1, k1] to last st, p1.
These 2 rows form single rib patt.
With C, work 3 rows in single rib.
With M, cont in single rib until scarf measures 90cm/35 ½in.
With right side facing, and using C, work 3 rows in single rib.
With M, work 3 rows in single rib.
Rep the first 10 cable rows of the patt 4 times.
Cast off in single rib.

AUGUST
SCARF

From left to right: **August Scarf** in Petal
(122) and Putty Grey (121), **August Scarf** in
Lilac Blossom (123) and Daisy Yellow (142),
August Scarf in Storm (102) and Seaside
(161) pattern on page 92

AUGUST SCARF

SKILL LEVEL **Beginner**

SIZES / MEASUREMENTS
To fit age   Baby   Toddler

ACTUAL MEASUREMENTS
Length	88	100	cm
	34 ½	39 ½	in
Width			
	10	12	cm
	4	4 ¾	in

MATERIALS
- 2(2) 50g/1 ¾oz balls of MillaMia Naturally Soft Merino in Lilac Blossom (123) (M).
- One ball contrast colour in Daisy Yellow (142) (C).
- Pair of 3.25mm (US 3) knitting needles.

TENSION / GAUGE
25 sts and 50 rows to 10cm/4in over g-st using 3.25mm (US 3) needles.

HINTS AND TIPS
This scarf is a satisfying quick knit in garter stitch that is a great introduction to colour work with the contrast colour border. Make sure you try to twist the yarn on the wrong side and in the same direction each time you switch colours to get a neat transition. You can also try using shorter needles (e.g. children's size needles) as this can make it easier to move the balls of yarn when switching colours.

ABBREVIATIONS
See page 9.

SUGGESTED ALTERNATIVE COLOURWAYS

Storm	Seaside	Petal	Putty Grey	Plum	Moss	Scarlet	Fawn
102	161	122	121	162	103	140	160

TO MAKE

Wind off half of C to make 2 equal size balls of C of approx 25g/⅞oz.
With 3.25 mm (US 3) needles and C cast on 24(30) sts.
1st row K to end.
2nd row K to end.
Cont in g-st for a further 6(8) rows.
Next row (right side) K4(5) C, change to M (twisting yarns on wrong side), k 16(20) M, join in another ball of C (again twisting yarns on wrong side) and k 4(5) C.
This row forms the patt.
Cont in patt until work measures 86.5(98)cm/34(38 ½)in, ending with a wrong side row.

Cut off M.
Next row With C, k to end.
Cont in g-st for a further 7(9) rows.
Cast off.
Sew in ends.

10 (12) cm
4 (4 ¾) in

88 (100) cm
34 ½ (39 ½) in

YARN COLOURS

Midnight
101

Storm
102

Moss
103

Claret
104

Forget
me not
120

Putty Grey
121

Petal
122

Lilac
Blossom
123

Snow
124

Scarlet
140

Grass
141

Daisy
Yellow
142

Fuchsia
143

Peacock
144

Fawn
160

Seaside
161

Plum
162

NOTES

NOTES

NOTES

INDEX

LILLEN BOTTOMS
page 60

LENA BLANKET
page 64

VIKTOR BLAZER
page 68

VIKTORIA CARDIGAN
page 72

KRISTINA PONCHO
page 78

ALEX PONCHO
page 82

ULLI HAT
page 86

ULLI SCARF
page 86

AUGUST SCARF
page 92

ABOUT MILLAMIA

We are two Swedish sisters living in London, who started MillaMia in 2009. Our Swedish heritage is hugely important to us. Having lived all over the world as we were growing up (including Singapore, USA and the UK) thanks to our father's job in an international company, the one constant we had was spending time every summer in Sweden. Eight weeks a year in the countryside of Sweden meant plenty of time to learn traditional crafts such as knitting to pass the time.

Our background influences the MillaMia style which is based on the distinctive Swedish aesthetic – clean and contemporary yet with a fun, bright edge. Qualities ideally suited to children's and baby wear.

As knitters we were frustrated by the patterns on offer for babies and children in the market today, and realising that there was a knitting renaissance underway, we saw a gap for stylish, modern baby and children's hand knitting patterns. Patterns that had a real design edge but still easy to knit and practical to use. Clothes that we would actually like to dress our kids, nieces and nephews in.

With Helena's background in fashion design we were able to do something about this gap in the market. Helena's designs are not constrained by conventional knitting or what has gone before. She takes account of current trends while at the same time directing our collections towards designs that you actually want to make and keep for years. This has allowed us to differentiate our patterns from what is already available today, and by working with the most experienced knitting technicians we have ensured that all the designs are suitable for hand knitting and manageable for most levels of knitters.

Finally a consideration of colour is at the centre of our design process. Carefully putting colours together that make the items really stand out. By producing our own MillaMia yarn, we have been able to select colours that are unique to our brand and put together colour combinations that really work – and that flatter babies and children.

Together these baby and children's knitting patterns and soft merino yarn form the core of the MillaMia product.

MillaMia is a family business and as such we believe in a friendly, personal service for all our customers. That is why we would really like to hear from you. If for any reason you are not one hundred percent happy with any of our items do get in touch. We see this as an opportunity to improve and want to make sure that you are entirely satisfied with your MillaMia purchase. We would also love to hear your ideas and what you are looking to knit next.

With best wishes,

Katarina and Helena Rosén
katarina@millamia.com or helena@millamia.com